CHRISTMAS HAUNTS
TRUE LEGENDS AND MYTHS

ETHAN HAYES

BEYOND
THE FRAY PUBLISHING

ISBN 13: 978-1-954528-95-6

Beyond The Fray Publishing
A division of Beyond The Fray, LLC
San Diego, CA

BEYOND
THE FRAY PUBLISHING

SINCE 2017

CONTENTS

INTRODUCTION

I remember the first time I heard a story about a Christmas ghost. I was sitting by the fireplace at my grandmother's old house, the smell of pine from the tree mingling with the warmth of wood smoke. Outside, snow blanketed the yard, and the world felt quiet, as if the earth itself had paused to listen. My grandmother, a woman who never missed a chance to share a good tale, leaned in close and told me about a spirit that roamed her village every Christmas Eve, leaving behind footprints in the snow that melted before dawn.

I was too young then to question whether such stories were true, but old enough to be captivated by the idea that the festive season—the time of joy, warmth, and family—could hold a darker, more mysterious side. As I grew older, I found myself drawn to these tales, searching for them in the dusty corners of libraries and in conversations with those who, like my grandmother, held a spark of belief in the unexplained.

And so, the idea for *Christmas Haunts* was born, a collection of stories from across the world where the spirit of the season takes on a spectral, eerie twist. These aren't the cozy fireside tales you might expect to hear on Christmas night. These are the stories whispered after the children are tucked in bed, when the house grows quiet, and the wind outside carries a strange, lonely howl. They are the accounts that keep us looking over our shoulders as we hang the wreaths, wondering if that flicker of shadow is just a trick of the light —or something more.

What struck me the most in compiling these stories was how deeply intertwined the supernatural is with the traditions of Christmas. For centuries, people have told ghost stories during the long winter nights, as if the darkness and the chill in the air somehow called out to the otherworldly. From the ancient Norse legends of the Wild Hunt, a spectral procession that rode through the sky during midwinter, to Victorian tales of restless spirits knocking on frosted windows, the season has always carried a hint of the uncanny. Even the famous line from *A Christmas Carol*, "There's more of gravy than of grave about you," hints at the long-standing tradition of ghostly encounters tied to the holiday.

During my research, I traveled from small towns in Wales to remote villages in Eastern Europe, spoke to witnesses who swore they had seen something inexplicable, and combed through local archives that held forgotten lore. Some stories were outright chilling—like the Jenkins family's strange encounter in Cwmbran, where the sound of sleigh bells on a snowless night heralded the arrival of something sinister. Others carried a touch of melancholy, like the story of a widow in the Scottish Highlands who claimed that her late husband's spirit would return every year to light a candle in their old cottage window.

Every account in this book has been shaped by those who experienced them, by the peculiarities of their towns, and by the traditions that shape how they understand the unknown. I have done my best to honor their stories, presenting them as they were told to me, with all their mystery intact. Some you may find impossible to believe; others might strike a chord deep within, stirring a sense of recognition you can't quite place.

For those of us who can't help but wonder what lies beyond the light of the Christmas tree, these stories offer a glimpse into a world where the cheer and the chill walk hand in hand. I can't promise you'll find answers here—most of the time, the people who lived through these tales couldn't either. But I hope that as you turn these pages, you'll feel the same shiver that I did when my grandmother first shared her story, the feeling that the night is never truly empty, even when all seems still.

So pour yourself a glass of mulled wine, settle into your favorite chair, and let these stories keep you company as the nights grow long and the air turns cold. After all, there's a certain magic to the darkness, and sometimes, if you listen closely, you might just hear the echoes of a story that refuses to rest.

—Ethan Hayes

CHAPTER ONE

THE CHRISTMAS EVE GHOST OF EASTERN STATE PENITENTIARY

Eastern State Penitentiary in Philadelphia, Pennsylvania, is one of the most notorious and haunted locations in the United States. Constructed in 1829, the prison was initially designed under the "Pennsylvania System" of solitary confinement, a reformist idea proposed by the Quakers. The goal was to inspire penitence through isolation, with each inmate housed alone in a small cell to reflect on their crimes.

While this system was meant to rehabilitate, it often led to madness, despair, and severe psychological trauma among prisoners. Over time, this grim atmosphere, combined with stories of brutal conditions, made Eastern State a prime site for tales of paranormal activity, including the famous Christmas Eve ghost.

Christmas celebrations in the penitentiary were stark and shadowed by the institution's bleak nature. Initially, prisoners spent Christmas alone in their cells, with small allowances like special meals. For much of the 19th century, Christmas inside Eastern State Penitentiary lacked the warmth and joy typically associated with the holiday. Instead of gatherings or decorations, inmates would receive simple meals of pork, potatoes, and a small amount of fruit. Many of them spent this time in utter solitude, forbidden from singing or speaking.

However, by the late 1800s, a shift occurred as carolers began visiting the penitentiary, bringing a rare moment of joy to the prisoners. The warden's journal entries from 1890 detail musical performances by bands, marking a significant break from the institution's earlier, more severe practices. These activities suggested a turning point in how the prison approached inmate well-being, but they were still far from the communal celebrations of freedom.

The tales of the Christmas Eve ghost at Eastern State are woven into the penitentiary's chilling atmosphere. One of the most enduring legends involves the spirit of a man believed to be a former guard or inmate, who appears on Christmas Eve each year. Accounts from visitors and tour guides report sightings of a spectral figure, shrouded in shadows, that paces the corridors of the old cellblocks during the night. This apparition is often seen near Cellblock 12, known for its intense paranormal activity, where whispers, shadowy figures, and inexplicable noises have been reported for decades.

Witnesses describe a chilling encounter with the ghost—a sudden drop in temperature, the sound of distant weeping or heavy footsteps, and an overwhelming sense of dread that accompanies sightings. Some believe that the spirit is a former guard who died tragically while on duty, while others speculate it is the restless soul of a prisoner who succumbed to despair during the Christmas season, a time when isolation and loneliness would have been particularly crushing.

Numerous stories from visitors and employees of the penitentiary tell of their brushes with the spectral figure on Christmas Eve. One such account comes from a maintenance worker named Gary Johnson, who experienced an eerie event in the 1990s while working to restore old locks. Johnson reported that as he struggled with a particularly stubborn lock, he felt a rush of cold air, followed by a paralysis that left him unable to move. He then witnessed faces materializing on the walls, accompanied by a deep sense of despair.

Other witnesses claim to have seen the shadowy figure standing silently in the ruins of the guard towers, which are now inaccessible due to crumbling stairways. These tales often share common elements: the bitter cold, the sensation of being watched, and disembodied voices that seem to float through the darkened hallways. For those who encounter the Christmas Eve ghost, the experience is unforgettable and profoundly unsettling.

The allure of the Christmas Eve ghost has drawn countless paranormal investigation teams to Eastern State, hoping to document the mysterious occurrences. Shows like *Ghost Hunters* and *Most Haunted* have filmed episodes at the penitentiary, capturing eerie phenomena on camera, including shadowy movements and unexplained noises. During these investigations, the teams have reported cold spots and malfunctions in their equipment, which some believe is a sign of the ghost's presence.

One theory about the ghost's origin suggests that it is the spirit of Joseph Taylor, a former inmate who committed a murder within the prison walls. Taylor, who killed an overseer in 1884, is believed to haunt the penitentiary, his rage and guilt anchoring him to the site. However, others think the Christmas Eve ghost might represent the collective suffering of many prisoners who died alone in their cells, their spirits drawn back to the penitentiary during the holiday season.

The connection between Christmas and ghostly activity at Eastern State is often attributed to the extreme loneliness experienced by prisoners during the holiday season. While families outside the prison celebrated, those inside faced a stark contrast—confined to solitary cells, with little more than a sparse meal to mark the occasion. The emotional weight of this isolation, combined with the penitentiary's brutal past, has left a profound mark on the building's energy.

Psychologists and paranormal enthusiasts alike have speculated that this emotional intensity contributes to the frequency of ghost sightings. The theories range from residual hauntings, where the intense emotions imprint themselves on the environment, to the more traditional concept of spirits trapped by unfinished business or trauma. The Christmas Eve ghost, therefore, could be seen as a manifestation of the collective sorrow of countless inmates who longed for freedom during a season meant for joy and togetherness.

The Christmas Eve ghost of Eastern State Penitentiary serves as a haunting reminder of the darker side of the holiday season. It is a story of longing and despair, set against the backdrop of one of America's most notorious prisons. As Eastern State has transformed into a museum and historical site, the stories of its spectral inhabitants continue to draw curious visitors each year, particularly those hoping to experience a brush with the otherworldly on Christmas Eve.

For those who visit, the penitentiary offers more than just a glimpse into the past; it offers a chilling encounter with a time when the holiday spirit was met with silence, solitude, and shadowy figures that still walk the halls. The ghost stories, like the one that plays out each Christmas Eve, are a testament to the enduring fascination with the mysteries of the human spirit, both in life and beyond.

CHAPTER TWO
THE DISAPPEARANCE OF THE SODDER
CHILDREN

On Christmas Eve of 1945, in Fayetteville, West Virginia, a fire destroyed the home of George and Jennie Sodder, changing their lives forever. Of the ten Sodder children, five vanished during the blaze, leaving behind a mystery that has endured for decades. The strange circumstances of the fire and the inconsistencies in the investigation led to lingering doubts, unsubstantiated theories, and a relentless quest for answers by the surviving family. Despite official conclusions, the Sodder family believed that their children had not died in the fire but had been abducted. This chapter delves into the events of that night, the aftermath, and the various theories that continue to surround the disappearance of the Sodder children.

The fire broke out around 1:00 a.m. on December 24, 1945. Jennie Sodder was awoken twice that night, first by a sound resembling something hitting the roof and then by the smell of smoke. She discovered the fire near the family's office and quickly roused George and the other children. In total, four children—Marion, Sylvia, John, and George Jr.—escaped the burning house with their parents. Despite their frantic efforts to call out to the five children sleeping upstairs— Maurice, Martha, Louis, Jennie, and Betty—no response came from the attic.

The family's attempts to rescue the remaining children were thwarted by a series of oddities. The ladder that George intended to use to reach the attic was missing, later found discarded in a nearby ditch. Attempts to start the trucks, which George hoped to use to reach the attic windows, were unsuccessful, even though they had worked perfectly the previous day. The nearby water barrel, which could have been used to combat the flames, was frozen solid. Unable to save their children, the family watched in horror as the house burned to the ground in less than an hour.

The Fayetteville Fire Department, despite being only 2.5 miles away, did not arrive until hours after the fire had reduced the house to ashes. The delay was attributed to a lack of manpower due to World War II and issues with the telephone lines, which were later found to have been cut rather than burned. By the time they arrived, there was little left but smoldering debris. The fire chief, F.J. Morris, initially suggested that the blaze was caused by faulty wiring. However, George and Jennie questioned this, noting that their Christmas lights remained on during the fire's early stages, something that would be unlikely if the fire had been electrical in nature.

The official investigation concluded that the children had perished in the fire, and death certificates were issued for them on December 30, 1945. Yet, no human remains were found in the aftermath, which puzzled both the family and outside experts. Jennie Sodder consulted with a local crematorium and learned that even at extremely high temperatures, bones should have survived the fire, especially since the house burned for less than an hour.

As doubts grew, George and Jennie began to believe that their children had not died in the fire but had been kidnapped. Suspicion was fueled by several peculiar incidents before and after the fire. Just months prior, a life insurance salesman warned George that his house would "go up in smoke" due to his outspoken anti-Mussolini views. Furthermore, a neighbor reported seeing a man stealing items from the Sodder property on the night of the fire, admitting later to cutting the phone lines. However, this lead was never pursued in detail by authorities.

In addition to these anomalies, several reported sightings of the Sodder children surfaced in the weeks following the fire. A woman claimed to have seen them in a car as the fire burned, and a hotel worker in Charleston, about 50 miles away, said she saw the children with two adults the morning after the blaze. These accounts described the children as being in the company of adults of Italian descent who appeared hostile when the hotel worker attempted to engage the children in conversation.

Refusing to accept the official version of events, George and Jennie launched their own investigation. They placed a large billboard along Route 16, offering a reward for information about their children and listing key questions about the inconsistencies in the investigation. The sign became a symbol of their quest for answers and remained there for decades, seen by passersby as a haunting reminder of the unsolved mystery.

The Sodders also hired private investigators, including C.C. Tinsley, who uncovered further oddities. Tinsley learned that Chief Morris had allegedly found an organ at the fire scene, which he buried in a box. Upon examination, this supposed organ turned out to be a piece of beef liver, untouched by fire. The suggestion was that Morris had planted it in an attempt to placate the grieving family. This revelation further deepened the Sodders' suspicions that authorities were covering up what really happened to their children.

In 1949, George Sodder hired Dr. Oscar B. Hunter, a patholo-gist from Washington, D.C., to conduct a more thorough search of the property. A few bone fragments were found, but analysis revealed that they belonged to someone much older than any of the missing children and showed no signs of exposure to fire. This fueled the family's belief that their children had been taken from the house before it burned.

Throughout the years, more tips and sightings trickled in, but none led to definitive answers. In 1967, Jennie received a photograph in the mail, purportedly of one of her missing sons, Louis. The man in the photo bore a striking resemblance to her son, now grown up. Despite hiring a private investigator to follow up on the lead, nothing concrete came of it. The investigator disappeared, adding another layer of mystery to an already convoluted case.

George Sodder passed away in 1969, and Jennie in 1989. Until her death, Jennie wore black as a sign of mourning, a testament to her undying hope that the truth about her children might still be uncovered. The surviving Sodder children and their descendants have continued to search for answers, maintaining that the case was never adequately resolved.

The disappearance of the Sodder children remains one of the most enduring mysteries in American true crime lore. The events of that Christmas Eve—marked by a rapidly spreading fire, missing ladders, failed rescue attempts, and conflicting accounts—have left more questions than answers. The Sodder family's persistent quest for the truth, despite societal pressures and dismissive authorities, speaks to their belief that their children might still have survived somewhere. While the official conclusion points to accidental death in a tragic fire, the evidence and lingering doubts suggest the possibility of a far more complex and sinister narrative. The Sodder children's story continues to haunt those who encounter it, serving as a chilling reminder that some mysteries remain unsolved, even as the decades roll on.

The family's tragic ordeal encapsulates the complexities of loss, the persistence of hope, and the painful search for truth amid conflicting evidence and unexplained events. Whether the children perished in the fire or were taken by unknown perpetrators, the mystery of the Sodder children endures as a haunting chapter in the annals of unexplained disappearances.

CHAPTER THREE
THE HAUNTED ROOM AT THE MYRTLES PLANTATION

The Myrtles Plantation, located in St. Francisville, Louisiana, is often referred to as one of the most haunted houses in America. Its history, steeped in the tragedies of its occupants and the injustices of slavery, has given rise to a multitude of ghost stories. Among these tales, the legend of Chloe, a former enslaved woman, stands out, intertwining with the eerie happenings that seem to peak around the holiday season, particularly Christmas.

The story of the Myrtles Plantation begins with General David Bradford, who built the original house in 1796. Bradford, known as "Whiskey Dave," fled Pennsylvania after being involved in the Whiskey Rebellion, seeking refuge in what was then Spanish-controlled Louisiana. He established a modest eight-room estate, which he named Laurel Grove. After receiving a presidential pardon, he was able to bring his family to the plantation, marking the start of a new chapter in the property's storied existence.

In 1817, Bradford's daughter, Sarah Matilda, married Clark Woodruff, a local law student who would later inherit and expand the plantation. Woodruff's management brought prosperity to the estate, but his family faced numerous hardships, including the deaths of Sarah and two of their children due to yellow fever. Over time, ownership of the plantation changed hands, and the name "Laurel Grove" was replaced with "The Myrtles" due to the crepe myrtle trees surrounding the property.

Among the numerous spirits rumored to inhabit the Myrtles Plantation, the tale of Chloe is the most enduring. According to legend, Chloe was an enslaved woman forced into a relationship with Clark Woodruff. Over time, she became fearful of losing favor and being sent back to the harsh labor of the fields. To prevent this, she allegedly began eavesdropping on the Woodruff family's conversations, hoping to secure her position. When caught listening in, she was punished severely—one version of the story claims her ear was cut off as a warning. After this, she wore a green turban to conceal the scar, a distinctive image that would later fuel ghostly sightings.

The story becomes even darker when Chloe is said to have poisoned a birthday cake with oleander, hoping to make the family ill so she could nurse them back to health and regain their trust. However, her plan backfired. Sarah Woodruff and two of her children died from the poison, while Clark remained untouched. After the deaths, Chloe was reportedly hanged by other enslaved people on the plantation, either out of fear of retribution or as a form of justice.

Though historical records do not support the existence of a woman named Chloe at the Myrtles, and many of the details of this story contradict documented events, the legend persists. Historians suggest that the deaths in the Woodruff family were more likely due to yellow fever than a sinister poisoning. Yet, this discrepancy has not dampened the belief that Chloe's spirit lingers at the plantation.

One room at the Myrtles, originally a dining room where the poisoning allegedly took place, has become a focal point for supernatural occurrences. This room, now referred to as the game room, is rumored to be a hotspot of eerie activity. It is said that the air grows cold and heavy, and those who enter the room sometimes hear the soft weeping of children or feel an unseen presence brush past them. Guests have reported seeing a woman in a green turban reflected in mirrors, even when no one is present. Some claim to have awoken in the dead of night to see Chloe's figure at the bedside, her face barely illuminated in the dim light.

Additionally, the plantation is home to other spectral legends. For instance, the spirit of William Winter, the victim of a documented murder in 1871, is said to relive his final moments within the house. After being shot on the front porch, he staggered up the stairs, only to collapse and die on the 17th step. To this day, the sound of heavy footsteps echoing through the halls is attributed to his restless spirit, forever replaying the tragic end of his life.

A Christmas Haunting

The legend of Chloe and the haunted room takes on a particularly haunting aura during the Christmas season. The plantation, with its moss-draped trees and creaking wood floors, is a stark contrast to the festive warmth associated with the holiday. Visitors often claim that supernatural events become more intense around this time of year. Theories suggest that the holiday season, with its emphasis on family and togetherness, might amplify the energies of those spirits who met a tragic end at the plantation.

Stories from guests and paranormal investigators speak of decorations being moved, Christmas lights flickering inexplicably, and soft whispers in empty rooms. The mirror, supposedly holding the spirits of Sarah Woodruff and her children, is often a source of strange phenomena, such as handprints appearing suddenly on its glass or figures seen only through its reflection. Some even report hearing the faint sound of children laughing, an eerie reminder of the young lives lost in the tale of the poisoned birthday cake.

While the stories of the Myrtles Plantation and its haunted room captivate visitors, many historians and skeptics question their authenticity. Research into the history of the plantation reveals discrepancies between the tales of Chloe and documented events. For instance, records show that Sarah Woodruff and her children likely died from yellow fever, not poisoning. Moreover, there is no evidence that the Woodruff family owned a slave named Chloe.

Yet, the persistence of these stories speaks to a deeper cultural memory, a need to understand and grapple with the profound tragedies of the past. The legend of Chloe, whether grounded in fact or purely fictional, serves as a narrative thread that links the horrors of enslavement and the eerie atmosphere that shrouds the plantation. It also offers a lens through which to view the broader history of the American South, where tales of spirits often reflect the region's painful legacies.

————

The Myrtles Plantation remains a popular destination for those seeking a brush with the supernatural. The haunted room, with its heavy history and the tales of Chloe's restless spirit, invites speculation and chills in equal measure. Whether driven by a belief in the paranormal or simply curiosity about the past, visitors to the Myrtles during the Christmas season often leave with stories of their own—unsettling encounters, inexplicable noises, or just a feeling that they were never truly alone during their stay.

In this way, the legend of the haunted room at the Myrtles Plantation endures, a ghost story that continues to be retold and reimagined, keeping alive the mysteries of a place where history and the supernatural seem to overlap. For those who believe, Christmas at the Myrtles is not just a time for celebration but a time when the veil between worlds grows thin, allowing glimpses of those who refuse to be forgotten.

CHAPTER FOUR
THE PHANTOM COACH OF BROCKLEY

Brockley, a quaint village in Suffolk, England, holds a chilling tale that has fascinated locals and intrigued visitors for generations. On the still, cold nights of Christmas Eve, whispers of a spectral presence drift through the village—an otherworldly coach drawn by headless horses, driven by a headless coachman. This eerie apparition, known as the Phantom Coach of Brockley, is said to glide through the snow-covered lanes, leaving behind the ghostly echo of hooves and creaking wheels.

The story has woven itself into the fabric of Brockley's folklore, blending elements of local history and the broader theme of spectral coaches found throughout English legends. Unlike more ordinary ghost tales, this one carries a specific dread—the appearance of the coach is seen as a harbinger of death, an omen that something dark lurks in the shadows of the festive season. While reports vary, the core details remain consistent: a black coach, headless figures, and the chilling atmosphere of a Christmas Eve encounter.

The exact origins of the Phantom Coach of Brockley are shrouded in mystery, with local storytellers tracing it back to the 18th century. Like many ghostly legends, it likely emerged from a blend of real historical events and the ever-present fear of the unknown. In the 1700s, the village would have been a quiet, isolated place, where the darkness of winter nights carried a particular weight, especially in the days leading up to Christmas.

Folklorists have speculated that tales of spectral coaches across England often stem from old superstitions surrounding death and the afterlife. Coaches, once symbols of wealth and status, became entwined with the supernatural, transforming into vehicles that ferried spirits between worlds. In Suffolk, the motif of a headless coachman further emphasizes the separation between life and death, as such figures were often seen as messengers of doom, delivering bad news or portending the death of someone in the community.

The most common retellings of the Brockley legend focus on sightings that occur around midnight on Christmas Eve. On these nights, the village streets are blanketed in snow, and a hush falls over the landscape. Those unlucky enough to cross paths with the phantom coach describe an experience that is both surreal and terrifying. It begins with the distant rumble of wheels and the rhythmic pounding of hooves, growing louder as the invisible carriage draws near.

Witnesses have reported a bone-chilling cold accompanying the sighting, as though the air itself freezes at the coach's approach. When the apparition finally becomes visible, it is a dreadful sight: a shadowy coach drawn by four horses, their heads missing, and a driver similarly decapitated, gripping the reins with a spectral determination. The coach's wheels do not leave tracks in the snow, and no breath steams from the horses, emphasizing its ghostly nature. As swiftly as it arrives, the coach disappears into the night, fading away until only the echoes of its passage remain.

The Phantom Coach of Brockley, like other tales of spectral coaches across England, serves multiple roles in local lore. On one hand, it acts as a reminder of mortality, appearing during a time of year that is traditionally associated with joy and celebration. The coach's appearance on Christmas Eve, a night symbolizing hope and renewal, introduces a stark contrast—transforming the cheerful into the chilling. The sight of a headless driver further evokes a sense of loss and detachment, symbolizing a soul that has lost its way.

In addition to being a death omen, the coach functions as a kind of supernatural watchman, patrolling the quiet lanes of Brockley as though guarding the boundaries between the living and the dead. Folklorists have compared it to similar tales from nearby counties, such as the ghostly coach of Roos Hall, Suffolk, which makes its rounds each year during the same season. Both stories reflect a deep-seated cultural fear of what lies beyond the veil of death and the possibility that, even after death, some souls continue to linger in the places they once knew.

One of the most famous accounts comes from the late 19th century, when a local farmer claimed to have encountered the coach while returning from a Christmas market. He described a surreal, freezing stillness before the sounds of the coach wheels reached him, and he saw the spectral vehicle pass right through a hedgerow without disturbing a leaf. Shaken, he shared his experience with villagers, who took it as a dire warning; not long after, a prominent member of the community passed away unexpectedly.

In the 1970s, a pair of travelers driving through Brockley on Christmas Eve reported seeing the shadowy outline of a coach crossing a moonlit field. They initially mistook it for an antique vehicle, part of a local celebration, but their confusion turned to fear when the coach vanished before their eyes. Many contemporary sightings have focused more on the eerie sounds rather than the visual manifestation, with reports of hoofbeats echoing through the empty village streets, even when no visible coach is present.

The legend of the Phantom Coach of Brockley has attracted various interpretations over the years. Some skeptics suggest that the sounds attributed to the coach could be caused by natural phenomena, such as shifts in the frozen ground or the cries of nocturnal animals. Yet, for believers, these rational explanations fail to account for the consistency and specificity of the sightings, particularly those that include visual elements.

Another theory is that the coach is a residual haunting, a kind of supernatural recording that replays a traumatic event. In this view, the coach and its headless occupants are trapped in a loop, endlessly retracing their route through Brockley. This aligns with similar stories in English folklore, where phantom coaches are often tied to tragic events or unfulfilled purposes. Perhaps the headless coachman of Brockley is doomed to drive through the village each Christmas Eve, bound to the roads he once traveled in life.

Local historians have also noted that the legend might have been influenced by the Wild Hunt, a mythological theme common in European folklore, where ghostly riders sweep through the countryside in pursuit of souls. The Phantom Coach, in this interpretation, serves as a smaller, localized version of this ancient belief, adapted to the specific landscape and history of Brockley.

The tale of the Phantom Coach remains an enduring part of Brockley's cultural identity, drawing interest from paranormal enthusiasts and folklore researchers alike. In recent years, local tours have occasionally focused on the ghostly tales of Suffolk, with the Brockley coach being a centerpiece of the storytelling. While sightings have become rarer, the legend's impact on the village's atmosphere is undeniable—visitors are often struck by the eerie quiet of Brockley's lanes, particularly in the winter months.

Residents have mixed feelings about their spectral fame. Some embrace the story as a charming piece of local heritage, while others regard it as a somber reminder of the unknown forces that may lurk beyond the edges of everyday life. For many, the coach represents a link between the past and present, an enduring mystery that refuses to be fully explained.

The Phantom Coach of Brockley is more than just a ghost story; it is a reflection of the fears and fascinations that have long gripped human imagination. On Christmas Eve, when the boundary between the living and the dead feels especially thin, the legend comes alive again in the minds of those who remember the stories. Whether the coach is a manifestation of supernatural forces or a collective echo of local history, it holds a powerful place in the lore of Suffolk.

Even now, on snowy winter nights, some still claim to hear the faint sound of wheels crunching through the snow, or the spectral echo of galloping hooves. And while few would admit to wanting to see the coach for themselves, the possibility lingers—adding a chill to the Christmas air in Brockley, Suffolk.

CHAPTER FIVE
THE CHRISTMAS EVE APPARITION OF
LORD TYRONE

The Christmas Eve apparition of Lord Tyrone to Lady Beresford is one of Ireland's most enduring and eerie ghost stories. It blends the elements of a childhood promise, the supernatural, and a chilling fulfillment of fate. At its core, the tale centers around the close relationship between John Le Poer, later Lord Tyrone, and Nichola Sophia Hamilton, who became Lady Beresford. Raised together as orphans, they were bound by a unique bond—a pact to prove the existence of the afterlife. This promise, made in their youth, would come to haunt Nichola on a fateful Christmas Eve, forever intertwining their destinies.

John Le Poer and Nichola Sophia Hamilton were brought up together after both became orphans in Ireland. Their guardianship fell to a fervent atheist who sought to dissuade them from belief in any form of afterlife. Despite this, the two children remained unconvinced and continued to harbor their own beliefs about the spiritual realm. They were particularly close, sharing the formative experiences of their childhood under the same roof, leading to a deep connection that would later play a pivotal role in the supernatural events that followed.

As teenagers, they made a pact: whichever of them died first would return to the other and confirm the existence of the afterlife. This promise was a solemn one, whispered between them as a guarantee that life did not end with death. Although life eventually separated them—Nichola married Sir Tristram Beresford and settled into the roles of a wife and mother, while John became Lord Tyrone—their bond remained strong, even beyond the grave.

The pivotal event of this story took place on Christmas Eve. By this time, John Le Poer, now Lord Tyrone, had passed away under mysterious circumstances. According to the account, Nichola, now Lady Beresford, awoke in the middle of the night to find her long-dead foster brother standing beside her bed. His presence was ethereal, shrouded in an otherworldly glow, and he reminded her of the promise they had made in their youth.

Lord Tyrone's apparition was not merely a manifestation of their pact; he brought with him a series of unsettling prophecies about Lady Beresford's future. He foretold that her husband would soon die, that she would remarry, and that she would bear four children. The most ominous of these revelations, however, was that she would die on the day she turned 47. The spirit's demeanor was somber, and Lady Beresford, shaken by the encounter, pressed him for proof that what she was experiencing was not a mere dream.

In response to her request for proof, Lord Tyrone's ghostly form reached out and took hold of her wrist. The touch of the apparition left an indelible mark; her wrist withered and shrank upon contact, a visible deformation that Lady Beresford carried with her for the rest of her life. This mark was a constant reminder of that night and the dark prophecy that accompanied it. From then on, she concealed her wrist with a black silk ribbon, a symbol of the spectral encounter she could never fully forget.

This physical sign served as a powerful testament to the reality of the apparition. Lady Beresford's insistence on wearing the ribbon, even in situations where it might raise questions, became one of the story's most haunting details. It suggested that the spirit's touch had left more than just a physical mark—it had left a psychological scar as well.

In the years following the apparition, Lord Tyrone's predictions began to unfold with eerie precision. Her husband, Sir Tristram Beresford, died not long after the ghostly visit. As foretold, Lady Beresford remarried and went on to have four children. Each event seemed to validate the encounter with the spirit, deepening her belief in the supernatural.

However, as her 47th birthday approached, Lady Beresford became increasingly anxious. She believed that the prophecy of her death on this particular day would come true. Yet, when she survived the day unscathed, she felt a fleeting sense of relief, thinking she had somehow escaped the fate that had been foretold. This relief was short-lived, however, as a critical revelation loomed over her celebrations.

On what she believed to be her 48th birthday, Lady Beresford gathered friends for a modest celebration. Among the guests was a clergyman who had been a close acquaintance of the family. During the gathering, she proclaimed her gratitude for having reached her 48th year, free from the curse of the prophecy. To her surprise, the clergyman corrected her, stating that she was, in fact, only 47, according to records he had recently reviewed.

The revelation hit Lady Beresford like a death knell. She realized that the prophecy still held sway, and in a moment of despair, she declared that the clergyman had signed her death warrant. True to the words of her foster brother's ghost, she withdrew to her chambers, made her final arrangements, and died that very night. Her death was seen as a confirmation of the spectral warning, cementing the legend of the Christmas Eve apparition as a tale of fate's inescapable grip.

The story of Lord Tyrone's apparition did not die with Lady Beresford. It was recorded by her granddaughter, Lady Betty Cobbe, and became a part of Irish folklore, preserved in manuscripts and family lore. Curraghmore House, where the story was recounted, became a site of intrigue, as visitors sought to understand the mystery of the black ribbon and the ghostly visitor who altered the course of a woman's life.

The tale embodies the themes of love, loyalty, and the supernatural, offering a narrative where the boundaries between life and death blur. It serves as a reflection of 17th-century beliefs in ghosts and the afterlife, as well as the cultural fascination with prophecies and fate. Today, it remains one of Ireland's most famous ghost stories, captivating those who hear it with its eerie promise of life beyond death and the grim fulfillment of a childhood vow.

The story of the Christmas Eve apparition of Lord Tyrone is more than a mere ghost story—it is a meditation on the inevitability of fate and the power of promises made in innocence. Through the figure of Lady Beresford, we see the weight of belief and the terror of knowing one's end long before it arrives. The spectral figure of Lord Tyrone continues to loom large in the annals of Irish folklore, a reminder that some bonds are too strong to be broken, even by death.

In the end, Lady Beresford's story is a chilling reminder that sometimes, the past reaches out with a spectral hand, leaving behind marks that cannot be concealed, even beneath a ribbon of silk. It is a story that has endured for centuries, retold by those who wonder at the thin veil between this world and the next—a veil that, on one Christmas Eve, parted just enough for a message from beyond.

CHAPTER SIX

THE GHOSTLY CHRISTMAS CAROLS OF EPWORTH RECTORY

The tale of Epworth Rectory's ghostly happenings stands among the most famous hauntings in England, rooted deeply in the lore of the Wesley family. The Rectory, built in 1709 in Epworth, Lincolnshire, became the home of Samuel Wesley, his wife Susanna, and their large family, including John and Charles Wesley, the founders of Methodism. The haunting that unfolded there in 1716-1717 is among the earliest and best-documented cases of poltergeist activity in Britain, with accounts that persisted for generations.

The events of this period coincided with the Christmas season, adding an eerie contrast to the festive time. It began with strange noises, unexplained footsteps, and mysterious knocks, but soon escalated into a haunting that gripped the entire Wesley family, the servants, and even the broader community. The spectral presence, later referred to as "Old Jeffrey," made the quiet rectory a place of fear rather than joy during the Christmas season.

The haunting of Epworth Rectory began in December 1716, just as winter set in and the air was filled with anticipation for the Christmas celebrations. The first signs of the supernatural came through faint, unexplainable sounds in the attic, particularly in the servants' quarters. The household staff, who initially dismissed these occurrences, soon faced louder and more disturbing phenomena—deep moans and rhythmic knocking that reverberated through the building, particularly at night.

Susanna Wesley, the matriarch, and her daughters began to hear these unsettling sounds as well. At first, Samuel Wesley, the rector, remained skeptical, attributing the noises to natural causes or the overactive imaginations of his children. However, when the sounds persisted and intensified, even Samuel could no longer ignore what was happening under his own roof.

As the haunting gained intensity, the figure behind the disturbances was given a name—Old Jeffrey. The family believed that Old Jeffrey could be the spirit of a former caretaker of the rectory, whose presence in the home seemed to grow stronger around Christmas. It is said that he made his presence known through knocks on walls, eerie footsteps that seemed to travel through the house, and even the sound of a ghostly trumpet.

Christmas at Epworth Rectory was typically a time for carols, prayers, and reflection, but the presence of Old Jeffrey turned the atmosphere from one of joy to trepidation. On several occasions, family members reported hearing what sounded like a disembodied voice mingling with the hymns they sang —an unearthly accompaniment that chilled them to the bone.

The Wesley family, devout Christians, struggled to reconcile their faith with the supernatural occurrences surrounding them. Susanna Wesley, known for her steadfast belief, initially tried to interpret the noises as divine tests or warnings, yet the consistency and physicality of the disturbances defied simple explanation. Letters from the Wesley daughters to their brother John, who was then studying at Oxford, detailed the disturbances in vivid terms. They wrote of objects being moved by invisible hands and rooms turning cold with no apparent cause.

The Christmas season in 1716 saw a surge in the paranormal activity. During the nights leading up to Christmas Day, the house seemed alive with spectral noises. There were reports of heavy thuds on the staircase, which Samuel Wesley interpreted as a warning or a prelude to some significant event. Some family members even experienced physical sensations, like being touched or pushed by unseen forces while praying or singing carols.

Christmas Eve at the rectory brought with it a particularly terrifying episode. As the family gathered for evening prayers, a loud, rhythmic knocking began to sound from the attic above. Samuel Wesley, determined to maintain the sanctity of the occasion, led the family in carols, hoping to drown out the sound. But as the hymns rose, so did the intensity of the noises, as if Old Jeffrey sought to assert his presence over the holy night.

Some accounts suggest that during this night, the disembodied sounds seemed almost musical, as though the ghost was trying to mimic or mock the carols being sung below. For a family steeped in religious tradition, the idea of a spectral presence participating in Christmas carols was both unnerving and deeply disturbing. Yet they continued their prayers, believing that their faith would protect them from the malevolent spirit.

The haunting at Epworth Rectory continued into early 1717, eventually subsiding as mysteriously as it began. By March, the strange noises and movements had nearly ceased, leaving the family to ponder what exactly they had experienced. John Wesley, who would later become a pivotal figure in Christian history as the founder of Methodism, remained intrigued by the events, using them as an example of the mysteries that lie beyond human understanding.

The legacy of the haunting has endured, becoming a subject of fascination for ghost enthusiasts, historians, and followers of the Wesleyan tradition. Many have speculated on the nature of Old Jeffrey—whether he was a restless spirit, a manifestation of the family's collective fears, or even a divine warning to the Wesleys. Regardless of the true cause, the story of the ghostly carols of Epworth Rectory remains a powerful reminder of how the supernatural can intertwine with human experiences, especially during times as emotionally charged as Christmas.

The haunting of Epworth Rectory raises important questions about the intersection of faith, fear, and the supernatural. For the Wesley family, devout Christians, the presence of a spirit in their home was not just a curiosity but a profound spiritual challenge. It forced them to confront the unknown and reconcile their experiences with their belief in a rational, orderly universe governed by divine will.

In later years, John Wesley would reflect on these experiences, using them as teaching moments in his sermons. He viewed the ghostly events at Epworth as evidence that there are forces beyond human comprehension—a belief that aligned with the early Methodists' openness to the mystical and the miraculous. The story of Old Jeffrey has since been woven into the broader narrative of the Wesley family, serving as a testament to their resilience and faith under extraordinary circumstances.

The ghostly happenings at Epworth Rectory are more than just a curious tale of supernatural phenomena—they are a window into the challenges and mysteries of life in early 18th-century England. At a time when Christmas was a deeply spiritual season, the intrusion of the ghostly into the festive celebration created a stark contrast that remains compelling to this day.

Whether viewed as a classic case of a poltergeist haunting or a psychological drama played out within the walls of a rectory, the story of Old Jeffrey has captured the imagination of those who hear it. It serves as a reminder that even during the brightest and most hopeful times of the year, there can be shadows lurking, waiting to make themselves known.

Today, Epworth Rectory stands as a historical site, where visitors can explore the home of the Wesleys and perhaps even sense a lingering presence in the cold corners of its attic. The story of Old Jeffrey, with his ghostly carols and unnerving manifestations, remains an integral part of the heritage of this storied place.

CHAPTER SEVEN
THE KNOCKING GHOST OF STOCKING FARM

In the late 17th century, amidst the quiet rural lands of Scotland, the Stocking Farm became infamous for one of the most disturbing cases of poltergeist activity in British history. The story of the Knocking Ghost of Stocking Farm weaves together folklore, superstition, and terrifying unexplained events that have persisted in local memory. This chapter delves into the chilling occurrences that plagued the Mackie family, the eyewitness accounts, and the attempts to exorcise the malevolent spirit that haunted this once-peaceful farmstead.

Stocking Farm, located near Ringcroft, was a modest rural farm tenanted by Andrew Mackie in the year 1695. The farm itself was unremarkable—a simple collection of stone buildings surrounded by fields. Yet, according to local lore, the area held a deeper, darker history. It was believed that a spectral presence lingered in the nearby woods, with locals often mentioning the "Ghost Tree," an old gnarled oak that was the last remnant of a long-gone forest. Superstition held that when this tree finally fell, the restless spirits tied to the land would rise again. This folklore set the stage for the mysterious and terrifying events that would soon unfold.

The disturbances at Stocking Farm began with a series of small but unsettling events. Andrew Mackie and his family noticed strange knocking sounds at night, echoing through the walls of their home. These knocks followed a peculiar rhythm, unlike any noise made by the house settling or animals outside. As the days passed, the phenomena escalated. Objects began to move on their own, doors would slam shut, and stones seemed to be thrown by unseen hands.

Soon, the farm was besieged by more aggressive manifestations. Witnesses, including neighbors and farm workers, reported seeing stones hurled through the air, seemingly without a source. Fires would ignite spontaneously, leaving the Mackie family and their neighbors in a state of fear and confusion. These events bore the hallmarks of a classic poltergeist haunting—noisy, violent, and malevolent.

One of the most terrifying aspects of the haunting was the appearance of a spectral figure—described as a young boy—seen wandering the grounds near the old Ghost Tree. Eyewitnesses recounted seeing this apparition just before a new wave of disturbances would begin. Unlike benign apparitions that merely appear and vanish, this entity seemed to carry with it an aura of malice, directly linked to the physical attacks that plagued the family.

Andrew Mackie and his family endured what could only be described as a campaign of terror. The unseen force would pelt them with stones, pull their hair, and even strike them with invisible hands. Mackie himself, a practical farmer, initially refused to believe in supernatural causes. But as the torment persisted, he turned to the local church, hoping for divine intervention.

Desperate to rid his family of this spectral torment, Andrew Mackie sought the help of Reverend Alexander Telfair, a respected clergyman known for his stern religious convictions and knowledge of folklore. Telfair arrived at Stocking Farm with a sense of skepticism but quickly found himself confronted by the reality of the situation. He documented his experiences meticulously, detailing the knocks, the objects thrown by unseen forces, and the strange cold that would fill a room just before an attack.

Reverend Telfair attempted a traditional exorcism, reading prayers and invoking the power of the Holy Trinity to banish the spirit. For a short time, the disturbances appeared to cease, and a sense of peace returned to Stocking Farm. But it was not to last. Within weeks, the knocking resumed, louder and more aggressive than before. This time, the spirit seemed even more malevolent, as if angered by the failed attempt to drive it away.

The haunting of Stocking Farm sparked debate and speculation among the locals and those who came to hear of it. Some believed that witchcraft was at the root of the problem, perhaps a curse placed on the land long before the Mackies arrived. Scotland, during this period, was rife with fear of witches, and accusations of sorcery could easily explain the mysterious phenomena in the eyes of 17th-century society.

Others proposed that the disturbances were the result of a tormented soul, perhaps the spirit of a child who had died under tragic circumstances. The boyish figure seen near the Ghost Tree lent credence to this theory. This explanation aligned with traditional ghost stories, where a spirit, bound to the place of its death, lashes out in confusion and anger. The spectral boy, coupled with the violent poltergeist activity, seemed to fit this pattern.

As time passed, the activity at Stocking Farm eventually diminished, but it never entirely vanished. Reports of knocks, sudden drops in temperature, and shadowy figures continued sporadically for years. The Mackie family, unable to fully escape the reputation of their haunted farm, eventually left the property. For generations, Stocking Farm remained uninhabited, a place where locals dared not tread after dark.

The legend of the Knocking Ghost of Stocking Farm became a part of the local folklore, a cautionary tale about the dangers of meddling with forces beyond human understanding. Even today, some claim that on cold, quiet nights, you can still hear the faint knocking echoing through the empty fields, as if the spirit of the boy and the malevolent force that once tormented the Mackies still linger on the land.

The story of the Knocking Ghost of Stocking Farm serves as a chilling reminder of the powerful grip that the supernatural holds over the human imagination. In the late 17th century, a simple farming family found themselves caught in a battle with forces they could neither understand nor control. The haunting left its mark not only on the Mackie family but also on the community that witnessed these terrifying events. Whether the disturbances were the result of a poltergeist, a cursed spirit, or something beyond comprehension, the tale of Stocking Farm endures as a classic ghost story that continues to captivate those with a taste for the macabre.

CHAPTER EIGHT
THE BROWN LADY OF RAYNHAM HALL

The Brown Lady of Raynham Hall is a renowned figure in the lore of English hauntings, her presence immortalized in one of history's most famous ghost photographs. Raynham Hall, located in Norfolk, England, is a stately home that dates back to the 17th century. The ghost, often identified as Lady Dorothy Walpole, has captivated the public imagination for centuries. The story of the Brown Lady is intertwined with tragedy, mystery, and a history of spectral sightings that have left even the most skeptical observers intrigued.

Dorothy Walpole, born in 1686, was the sister of Sir Robert Walpole, who is widely considered Britain's first Prime Minister. Dorothy's life took a dramatic turn when she became entangled with Charles Townshend, whom she eventually married. Townshend, known for his fiery temper and political prowess, was not an ideal husband. Their marriage was reportedly strained, with whispers of infidelity and disputes. Some accounts suggest that Charles imprisoned Dorothy within Raynham Hall after discovering an affair with Lord Wharton.

Dorothy's life within Raynham Hall became one of isolation. Deprived of contact with the outside world and her children, she is said to have fallen into despair. In 1726, she died under mysterious circumstances. While the official cause of death was smallpox, rumors persisted that she may have been locked away, her tragic story setting the stage for her to become the restless spirit known as the Brown Lady.

The first recorded sighting of the Brown Lady dates back to Christmas of 1835, during a gathering at Raynham Hall. Colonel Loftus and a fellow guest, Hawkins, encountered the apparition while heading to their rooms. Loftus described a woman dressed in an old-fashioned brown dress, her face glowing eerily but lacking eyes—only empty sockets remained. This unsettling vision was soon followed by more reports, solidifying the presence of a spectral figure that came to be known as the Brown Lady.

A year later, in 1836, Captain Frederick Marryat, a naval officer and author, requested to spend the night in the haunted quarters of Raynham Hall to validate the rumors himself. During his stay, Marryat reportedly encountered the Brown Lady carrying a lantern. Fearing for his life, he fired his pistol at the ghostly figure, but the bullet passed through her and embedded itself in the door behind. Marryat's experience only heightened the lore surrounding Raynham Hall's most famous resident, leading to further tales of encounters and eerie phenomena.

On September 19, 1936, the most famous incident involving the Brown Lady occurred when Captain Hubert C. Provand and his assistant, Indre Shira, were photographing Raynham Hall for *Country Life* magazine. As they prepared to take a shot of the grand staircase, Shira noticed a misty form descending the stairs and directed Provand to capture the image. The photograph that emerged became a sensation, showing a translucent figure gliding down the staircase, shrouded in a white, veil-like mist.

The photograph, published in *Country Life* and later in *Life* magazine, quickly became a subject of fascination and debate. Paranormal investigator Harry Price, who interviewed the photographers, found their story convincing and the photograph free from signs of tampering. Nonetheless, skeptics proposed alternative explanations, including double exposure, photographic smudging, or deliberate trickery. Despite the doubts, the photograph remains one of the most compelling pieces of supposed evidence for the existence of ghosts, keeping the legend of the Brown Lady alive.

Even after the famous photograph, sightings of the Brown Lady continued, though less frequently than in earlier years. Visitors to Raynham Hall reported feeling a chill in the air and seeing glimpses of a woman dressed in antiquated attire, moving through the shadows of the house. Others have claimed that her spirit may have moved to nearby estates like Houghton Hall, suggesting that the restless nature of the Brown Lady is not confined to Raynham Hall alone.

The Brown Lady is often described as a full-bodied apparition, though her appearances are accompanied by an air of sorrow. Witnesses consistently recount the unsettling emptiness of her eye sockets, an image that has left a deep impression on those who have claimed to encounter her. These stories, combined with the haunting photograph, have made the Brown Lady a significant figure in British ghost lore, inspiring numerous books, television programs, and ghost tours.

The story of the Brown Lady has inspired many interpretations, both supernatural and mundane. Believers assert that her spirit lingers due to the tragic circumstances of her life and untimely death. They suggest that she cannot find peace, bound to the halls where she experienced so much suffering. The story of Dorothy's mistreatment and possible imprisonment lends a certain credibility to the idea of a troubled spirit, especially given the intense emotions that may have surrounded her final days.

Skeptics, on the other hand, offer more practical explanations. They argue that the sightings and the famous photograph might be attributed to pareidolia, where the human mind perceives familiar patterns, like faces, in random stimuli. The photograph itself has been scrutinized as a potential double exposure, a common issue with cameras of the time, or even a simple case of lighting anomalies. Others believe that Indre Shira's enthusiasm for capturing the ghost may have influenced the account.

The enduring fascination with the Brown Lady of Raynham Hall speaks to a broader human interest in the unknown and the possibility of life after death. The story taps into the Victorian era's obsession with the supernatural, which persisted well into the 20th century. As tales of haunted houses, spectral figures, and cursed family histories gained popularity, the Brown Lady stood out as a vivid and tragic figure.

Raynham Hall itself has become a destination for those intrigued by the paranormal. The house's grand architecture, with its shadowy corridors and historic ambiance, provides a fitting backdrop for the legend of the Brown Lady. Over time, the story has been woven into the very identity of the estate, making it a place where history and folklore converge.

The legend of the Brown Lady of Raynham Hall endures because it embodies the intersection of history, tragedy, and the unexplained. Whether viewed as a symbol of Dorothy Walpole's suffering or a fabrication of overactive imaginations, her story continues to captivate those who hear it. The haunting photograph, mysterious sightings, and chilling accounts have solidified the Brown Lady's place in the annals of ghostly legends. As long as Raynham Hall stands, the spectral figure of the Brown Lady will remain a part of its lore, a reminder of how the past can linger in unexpected ways.

While definitive proof of her existence remains elusive, the Brown Lady's story has become a part of British cultural heritage, representing the mysteries that dwell at the edge of history and the supernatural. Through her tale, Raynham Hall remains not just a stately home, but a place where the past refuses to fade entirely into memory, making it a quintessential site for those fascinated by the ghostly and the unknown.

CHAPTER NINE
THE GHOST OF SIR CHRISTOPHER WREN'S CHURCH

St. Paul's Cathedral

Nestled within the ancient streets of London, the Church of St. James Garlickhythe stands as a testament to the city's resilient spirit and rich history. Rebuilt by Sir Christopher Wren after the Great Fire of London in 1666, the church has become known for its distinctive architecture, earning the nickname "Wren's Lantern" due to its abundance of windows that fill the interior with light. But beyond its architectural beauty and historical significance, the church harbors a haunting story—one that surfaces every Christmas Eve, attracting both curious visitors and devoted parishioners.

Every year, as the city of London winds down for Christmas, the church of St. James Garlickhythe prepares for a spectral visitor. Local legend speaks of a ghostly figure, believed to be a former sexton, who returns to the church each Christmas Eve. His appearance is not menacing but rather melancholic, as he seems to relive the duties he performed in life. He sweeps the aisles and tidies the pews, much like he might have done centuries ago when the church was bustling with activity.

St. James Garlickhythe

This spectral figure is often described as a shadowy, indistinct form that moves methodically through the church's interior. Witnesses who have seen the ghost claim that he fades into the darkness when approached, vanishing without a trace. Unlike more ominous hauntings, this one carries a sense of sorrow and duty, as if the ghost is bound to maintain the sanctity of the space even in death.

The history of St. James Garlickhythe adds layers of intrigue to the story of its haunting. The site's religious history dates back to the 12th century, but it was devastated by the Great Fire of London. Sir Christopher Wren, the eminent architect behind the reconstruction of St. Paul's Cathedral and numerous other London churches, took on the challenge of rebuilding it. Wren's version of the church, completed in 1683, featured a striking combination of brick and Portland stone, with a tower that has since become an iconic part of the London skyline.

The church's location near Garlick Hill contributed to its name—derived from the medieval garlic trade that once thrived along the banks of the Thames. The church's history includes ties to many influential figures, such as the composer William Boyce, who was baptized there, and six Lord Mayors of London, whose plaques adorn the church's walls.

The ghost that roams St. James Garlickhythe is believed to be the spirit of a former sexton, though his exact identity remains a mystery. The role of a sexton traditionally involved maintaining the church's grounds, ringing the bells, and keeping the building clean—a job that connected them deeply to the physical space of the church. In the 18th and 19th centuries, sextons were an integral part of church life, ensuring that the sanctuary remained a welcoming place for worshippers.

Some speculate that the ghost could be connected to one of the church's more macabre discoveries: the mummified body known as "Jimmy Garlick," unearthed in the 19th century during renovations. While the mummy itself is not directly associated with the Christmas Eve ghost, its presence has fueled tales of lingering spirits within the church. Jimmy Garlick is now housed within the church, adding to its mysterious atmosphere and drawing those interested in the paranormal.

The haunting of St. James Garlickhythe is made all the more evocative by the church's atmosphere during the Christmas season. On Christmas Eve, the church is often filled with candlelight and the echoes of carols reverberating through the high nave. As the city outside quiets down, the ancient stone walls of the church seem to come alive with memories of centuries past.

Those who have encountered the ghost speak of a sudden chill in the air, a moment when the bustling warmth of the season gives way to an eerie stillness. Some parishioners believe that the sexton returns out of a sense of devotion— continuing to care for the church as he did in life. Others see his presence as a reminder of the church's long history, a connection between the living and the dead that endures within the sacred space.

The story of the ghostly sexton has inspired numerous interpretations over the years. For some, it represents the lingering energy of the past—a manifestation of the countless prayers and rituals that have taken place within St. James Garlickhythe's walls. The idea of a spirit lingering to maintain the order of a holy place is a common theme in folklore, emphasizing the sacredness of the church as a space of continuity between life and death.

Others believe the sexton's appearance is more symbolic, perhaps representing the endurance of tradition and the unbroken line of caretakers who have served the church over the centuries. The ghost's presence during the Christmas season, a time of reflection and remembrance, might be seen as a reminder of the many generations who have worshiped at St. James Garlickhythe, their lives intertwined with the story of the church.

In recent years, the ghost of St. James Garlickhythe has become a part of the church's identity, attracting both those curious about the supernatural and those drawn to the rich history of Wren's architectural masterpiece. The story of the sexton has been passed down through oral tradition, with each retelling adding to the lore. While many modern visitors come seeking a glimpse of the ghost, others find themselves captivated by the church's serene beauty and the sense of history that pervades every corner of the building.

The church, with its ancient records, its connection to the past, and its tales of the supernatural, serves as a unique portal into London's layered history. The legend of the ghostly sexton is just one part of its story, but it is a part that captures the imagination—evoking the sense that even in a city as dynamic as London, the past is never truly gone.

The ghost of the sexton at St. James Garlickhythe is more than just a tale of a spectral figure; it is a reminder of the enduring spirit of a place where history and faith have intertwined for centuries. Each Christmas Eve, as the ghost quietly goes about his spectral duties, he serves as a symbol of devotion that transcends time. For those who gather in the church during this special season, his presence is a reminder that even as the world changes, some bonds remain unbroken, and some spirits, like those of London's past, continue to linger in the shadows of its storied buildings.

CHAPTER TEN
THE MISTLETOE BRIDE

Bramshill House in Hampshire

The tale of the Mistletoe Bride is one of the most haunting and enduring legends of England, weaving together elements of love, tragedy, and the supernatural. This story, dating back to at least the 16th century, centers on a young bride who meets a tragic end during her wedding festivities, becoming forever intertwined with the lore of Christmas and haunted manor houses. The story is often linked to Bramshill House in Hampshire, but similar tales have been told at various estates across England, each claiming their own spectral bride. Yet, no matter where it is recounted, the essence remains the same: a game of hide-and-seek that ends in terror, leaving a bride entombed in a chest, her spirit doomed to wander in search of release.

The legend begins with a Christmas wedding, a celebration that blends the joy of matrimony with the festive cheer of the holiday season. At the heart of this story is a young bride, sometimes named Anne or Genevre, who is said to have married a nobleman at a grand manor—often identified as Bramshill House, a Jacobean estate in Hampshire. According to one version, the newlyweds sought to make their celebration memorable with a game of hide-and-seek.

The groom and guests, filled with merriment, agreed to the bride's suggestion, not knowing the darkness that would soon overshadow their joy. As the game commenced, the bride slipped away, her white gown trailing behind her as she hurried through the manor's winding corridors. She sought the perfect hiding place, a spot so secretive that it would take her new husband hours to find her. In an attic room, she came across a large oak chest, old and dusty, yet sturdy enough to hide her from view. With a mischievous smile, she climbed inside, clutching a sprig of mistletoe in her hand—symbolic of the season's blessings.

As the lid of the chest closed, it sealed with a heavy thud, unbeknownst to the bride that the latch had locked automatically. She had no way of knowing that this simple game would become a fight for her life. Minutes turned to hours as the groom and guests searched for her throughout the manor, calling her name, their shouts mingling with the crackling warmth of the Christmas fire. But the bride's own cries, muffled within the chest, could not penetrate the thick wooden walls.

Over time, the celebration turned to confusion, then to panic as the hours passed and the bride remained unfound. Yet, it wasn't until many years later—sometimes the stories claim fifty years—that the chest was finally opened. Inside, the skeletal remains of the young bride were discovered, still adorned in her decayed wedding dress, clutching the withered mistletoe. Her death had been slow and suffocating, a grim testament to the cruel twist of fate that had turned a joyous celebration into a story of horror.

The legend of the Mistletoe Bride is intimately tied to Bramshill House, a manor known for its many ghostly tales. Situated in Hampshire, Bramshill House is a grand Jacobean estate built between 1605 and 1612. It is said to be home to numerous specters, including the so-called "White Lady," believed by many to be the spirit of the ill-fated bride. Those who claim to have encountered her describe a figure in white, sometimes glimpsed passing through darkened hallways or lingering near the chest that sealed her fate. Some have reported hearing faint, heart-wrenching cries echoing through the manor late at night—a spectral echo of the bride's last, desperate attempts for freedom.

The chest itself, or a replica of it, is displayed in the house's entrance hall, a grim reminder of the tragic event. It has become an object of morbid fascination for visitors, many of whom claim to feel a sudden chill when they approach it. The legend persists that each Christmas, the bride's spirit returns, drawn back to the scene of her death, searching for peace that eludes her even in death.

While Bramshill House is the most famous setting for the Mistletoe Bride's story, the legend has been attributed to other English manors as well, each claiming to be the origin of the tale. These include Marwell Hall in Hampshire and Minster Lovell Hall in Oxfordshire. The recurring nature of this legend in various locations suggests that it taps into deeper fears and motifs of Gothic storytelling—loss, entrapment, and the spectral presence of a life cut short.

The tale became especially popular in the Victorian era, a time when ghost stories were a staple of Christmas traditions. Writers like Thomas Haynes Bayly and poets of the era immortalized the Mistletoe Bride in verse, capturing the sorrow of a young woman trapped in her "living tomb". These stories were later adapted into plays, songs, and even early silent films, each retelling carrying the same chilling refrain: a bride who vanished on her wedding night, her fate discovered only when it was too late.

Beyond the immediate tragedy, the legend of the Mistletoe Bride carries layers of symbolism. Mistletoe, a plant associated with fertility, protection, and the renewal of life, contrasts sharply with the story's ending—a bride whose life is cut short in the most horrific manner. The image of the mistletoe in her hand, withered alongside her decayed form, suggests a dark inversion of the usual festive connotations of the plant. This lends the tale an eerie poetic quality, making it resonate deeply with those who hear it.

The chest, a domestic object meant for safekeeping, transforms into a tomb—a symbol of how safety can turn to peril when fate intervenes. This element of unexpected danger within the familiar is a classic theme in Gothic literature, reminiscent of Edgar Allan Poe's tales of premature burial and the unpredictability of life.

The Mistletoe Bride's story endures because it encapsulates the intersection of love and death, joy and sorrow, all under the shadow of a holiday that celebrates both togetherness and reflection. Each year, as the story is retold during the Christmas season, it serves as a reminder of the thin line between life's pleasures and its hidden dangers. Visitors to Bramshill House, and others who come across the legend, are left with the image of a young woman trapped forever in her bridal attire, a spectral figure who moves silently through the halls in search of a release she can never find.

The power of this tale lies not only in its macabre details but also in its timelessness. It is a story that has been told around firesides and in drawing rooms for centuries, keeping alive the memory of a tragic bride who sought only a moment of playfulness and found, instead, a lonely and bitter end. And so, as the mistletoe is hung each holiday season, the shadow of the Mistletoe Bride lingers, a ghostly echo from a past that refuses to be forgotten.

CHAPTER ELEVEN
THE GHOST OF ANNE BOLEYN AT CHRISTMAS

Portrait of Lady Anne Boleyn

Hever Castle, nestled in the serene Kent countryside, carries a legacy steeped in Tudor history and legend. Among its many stories, the most enduring is that of Anne Boleyn, the ill-fated second wife of King Henry VIII. The castle, once her childhood home, becomes the stage for a spectral appearance each Christmas. Legend has it that Anne's ghost returns during the holiday season, wandering the grounds she once knew so well. This chapter explores the history, legends, and eerie tales that surround Anne Boleyn's ghost at Hever Castle, especially her connection to Christmas, a time filled with both joy and melancholy for her memory.

Hever Castle

Hever Castle's history stretches back to 1270, but its significance grew after being acquired by the Boleyn family in the 15th century. Anne Boleyn spent much of her early life here, surrounded by the rich tapestry of Tudor life and courtly ambitions. The castle's double moat, stone halls, and sprawling gardens held memories of a carefree youth before her fateful involvement with King Henry VIII. Hever's history is interwoven with the story of a young woman whose ambitions would reshape the course of English history and whose tragic end has, in folklore, kept her spirit tethered to this ancient place.

Anne Boleyn's story is one of the most tragic in English royal history. Her marriage to Henry VIII was initially marked by the king's fervent desire to secure her as his queen. But the relationship, once full of hope, soured after Anne failed to produce a male heir, giving birth instead to Elizabeth I. Henry's love turned to disdain, and Anne's downfall was swift. Accused of treason, adultery, and incest, she was imprisoned and executed at the Tower of London on May 19, 1536. Her death marked a turning point in English history, but it also began a series of ghostly tales and sightings that would emerge over centuries.

Each year around Christmas, Hever Castle becomes the setting for eerie tales of Anne's return. It is believed that her spirit, draped in shadows, appears on Christmas Eve, gliding across the grounds she once roamed as a child. The most famous sightings occur around the large oak tree on the estate, where it is said that she and Henry courted in their youth. Here, her ghostly form is sometimes seen beneath the branches, reflecting on a time of promise and courtship, a stark contrast to her later tragic fate.

One particularly evocative story describes Anne's apparition crossing the bridge over the River Eden, which flows through the castle grounds. Witnesses describe her as moving silently across the bridge, sometimes pausing as if gazing into the water. According to the legend, she occasionally tosses a sprig of holly into the river, a gesture that might symbolize a longing for peace or a reflection on lost dreams. As the holly drifts away, her spectral form fades into the mist, leaving behind an air of mystery and sorrow.

Why does Anne's spirit appear during the Christmas season? For Anne, Hever Castle was not just a home; it was a place of sanctuary during her youth and a refuge during difficult times. Christmas in Tudor England was a grand affair, filled with feasts, revelry, and family gatherings. It is thought that Christmas might have held special significance for Anne, a time when the warmth of family gatherings contrasted sharply with the cold isolation she later faced in the Tower of London. Her spirit's return during the festive season could be a reflection of this longing for the joy and warmth she once experienced at Hever.

Moreover, Christmas itself in Tudor times had a deeply spiritual significance, blending elements of Christian devotion with older, more mystical beliefs about the veil between the living and the spirit world. Such beliefs may explain why ghosts are said to be more active during this time, and Anne's spirit is no exception, making her presence felt when the season's energy is at its peak.

Over the years, many visitors and staff at Hever Castle have reported encounters with Anne's ghost during the holiday season. Some describe a soft, mournful presence that lingers in the air, while others claim to have seen her spectral form in full Tudor dress, moving gracefully through the gardens or pausing near the castle's historic oak tree. One account speaks of a visitor who, during a late-night walk in the gardens, felt an inexplicable chill and turned to see a faint figure by the river, draped in shadows, before it vanished as suddenly as it had appeared.

These stories have become part of Hever's Christmas lore, attracting those curious about the supernatural. The castle's ambiance, with its candle-lit rooms and the quiet hush of winter, creates the perfect backdrop for tales of Anne's ghost. Christmas decorations at Hever include traditional Tudor wreaths and garlands, enhancing the sense of stepping back into Anne's time, where her presence seems to linger just beyond the edge of reality.

Tower of London

While Hever Castle is the heart of Anne's Christmas hauntings, her spirit is not confined to Kent. Other locations tied to Anne's life and death, such as the Tower of London and Blickling Hall in Norfolk, also claim to witness her ghostly visits. At Blickling Hall, it is said that her headless ghost returns each year on the anniversary of her execution, carried in a spectral carriage driven by a headless coachman. Yet, these manifestations are far more somber and macabre

than the peaceful, if melancholic, presence that graces Hever
during the Christmas season.

Blickling Hall in Norfolk

The stories of Anne Boleyn's ghost at Hever Castle reflect a
broader human fascination with the past and the desire for
closure. Anne's return each Christmas can be seen as a
yearning for the peace that eluded her in life. Her presence at
Hever, rather than evoking fear, seems to offer a quiet
reminder of her enduring connection to a place where she
once experienced love and hope. For many, the ghost of Anne
Boleyn is not just a supernatural tale but a symbol of the
lingering emotions and unfinished business that history
leaves behind.

The legend of Anne Boleyn's ghost at Christmas adds a
haunting, yet poignant dimension to Hever Castle's rich
history. Her story, woven into the fabric of the castle's past,
continues to intrigue and inspire those who visit, especially

during the holiday season. In a place where the past is always present, Anne's ghost serves as a reminder of love, loss, and the enduring power of memory. As visitors gather at Hever each year to celebrate the season, they also pay silent homage to the restless spirit of a queen who changed history, yet found a kind of eternal presence in the place she once called home.

CHAPTER TWELVE
THE GHOSTLY CAROL SINGERS OF CORNWALL

Nestled in the rolling hills of eastern Cornwall, the ancient town of Launceston has long been known for its rich history, marked by medieval architecture, historic conflicts, and folklore that seems to linger in the cobbled streets. Among these stories, one spectral tale has captured the imagination of locals and visitors alike—the legend of the ghostly carol singers. Each year, as December frost blankets the town, ethereal voices can be heard singing traditional carols, but no one can ever find the source. This chilling yet enchanting phenomenon has become part of Launceston's winter lore, intertwining with the town's centuries-old customs and its deep-rooted connection to the supernatural.

The origins of the ghostly carol singers are unclear, with different versions of the story circulating through local tales and historical anecdotes. Some believe the spectral carolers are the spirits of a long-lost choir, possibly a group of parishioners who perished during a harsh winter or a tragic event, such as a plague outbreak that swept through the town in the 17th century. According to this version, the singers were devoted churchgoers who found solace in hymns and carols, even during the darkest times. Their souls, unable to rest, return each year, filling the night air with their otherworldly voices, singing the same carols they once loved.

Another version suggests a connection to the town's history of Catholic persecution. Launceston was a site of significant religious turmoil during the Reformation. The martyrdom of St. Cuthbert Mayne in 1577—executed for his Catholic beliefs —is a prominent part of the town's past. Some locals whisper that the carolers are the spirits of Catholic faithful who met their end for defying religious orders. Their songs are a form of defiance, a reminder of their suppressed faith, echoing through the winter nights.

For those who venture into Launceston during the holiday season, the ghostly carolers add a mysterious charm to the town's festive atmosphere. As twilight falls and a chill settles over the town, residents and tourists have reported hearing faint melodies drifting down from the castle ruins or through the narrow alleys near the ancient churches. The songs are always traditional—"God Rest Ye Merry, Gentlemen," "Silent Night," and "The Holly and the Ivy"—but the voices have a distant, unearthly quality, as if carried by the wind from another time.

Many have attempted to track down the source of these haunting harmonies. Guided by curiosity, listeners have followed the sound through the winding streets, only to find themselves standing alone in a silent square, the music abruptly gone. The echoes seem to come from nowhere and everywhere at once, fading just as quickly as they appear. Local historians have suggested that the town's acoustics, shaped by its medieval architecture, might play tricks on the ears, but no explanation has ever fully accounted for the phenomenon.

Launceston's ancient buildings and narrow passageways create a perfect setting for the ghostly tales that have grown around the town. Its Norman castle, a remnant from the 11th century, stands as a sentinel over the town, its shadowy ruins often cited as a hotspot for paranormal activity. The Southgate Arch, one of the few remaining medieval gates, adds to the town's eerie charm. These landmarks, combined with the old churchyards and stone cottages, make it easy to imagine spectral figures wandering through the misty streets, their voices carried on the winter wind.

Some locals believe that the ghosts of the carolers use these very streets and buildings to amplify their songs, creating an otherworldly soundscape that is difficult to pinpoint. The resonance of voices against stone, they claim, allows the carolers to move unseen, transforming the town into a vast, open-air concert hall where time itself blurs.

Stories from locals add weight to the legend. One account comes from a shopkeeper who swore he heard carols late one night as he was closing up for the evening. The sound seemed to come from St. Mary Magdalene Church, yet when he went to investigate, he found the church locked and dark. Another tale tells of a group of carolers in the 1920s who, while singing on Christmas Eve, suddenly heard a chorus join them in perfect harmony. But when they paused to thank the mysterious newcomers, they found themselves singing alone on the empty street.

Even more recent stories have circulated among the town's ghost tours, which are popular during the colder months. Paranormal enthusiasts flock to Launceston, hoping for a chance to hear the spectral songs for themselves. Some claim to have recorded faint music on their phones, though skeptics attribute this to wind or distant echoes. Nevertheless, these encounters have become a significant part of Launceston's Christmas lore, drawing those intrigued by the possibility of a genuine brush with the supernatural.

The ghostly carol singers of Launceston are often discussed within the broader context of Cornish folklore, which is steeped in tales of spirits, pixies, and ancient rites. Cornwall's reputation as a mystical region is well-deserved; the land itself is seen as a place where the veil between the worlds is thin. Launceston, with its deep history and tragic past, becomes a perfect backdrop for stories of restless spirits.

Local folklorists have proposed that the carol singers could be part of a collective memory—echoes of past Christmas celebrations that have somehow become imprinted on the town's atmosphere. This theory, often referred to as a "stone tape" phenomenon, suggests that intense emotions or events can leave behind a sort of recording, which replays under the right conditions. In Launceston's case, the carols could be a manifestation of the town's festive past, surfacing each year like a song stuck on repeat.

Others see a more spiritual explanation. To some of Launceston's residents, the ghostly carolers represent a message from the past, reminding the living of the importance of community, tradition, and remembrance. In a world where time often moves too quickly, these spectral voices urge listeners to pause, listen, and reflect on the history that has shaped their town.

The legend of the ghostly carolers has become an integral part of Launceston's cultural fabric. Every December, it is discussed in the town's pubs, featured in local folklore events, and woven into storytelling sessions at community gatherings. It has even inspired some of the town's artists and poets, such as Charles Causley, whose work frequently draws on Cornwall's supernatural heritage. The story brings a sense of wonder to the holiday season, enriching the town's atmosphere with a feeling that anything is possible on a winter's night.

The legend also serves as a connection between generations. Older residents recount the tales they heard from their grandparents, while younger generations add their own experiences, keeping the story alive and evolving. In this way, the ghostly carolers of Launceston are more than just a story—they are a living part of the town's identity, a reminder of its deep connection to the past.

The ghostly carol singers of Launceston remain an enduring mystery, a story that combines the magic of Christmas with the allure of the supernatural. Whether they are spirits of long-dead parishioners, echoes from another time, or something beyond human understanding, their haunting melodies continue to enchant and mystify those who hear them. As long as Launceston endures, so too will the legend of the carolers—a timeless reminder that the past is never as distant as it seems, especially on cold December nights when the air is filled with the sound of voices that may not be of this world.

In this ancient town where history and folklore intertwine, the ghostly carolers serve as a bridge between the living and the dead, between tradition and mystery, ensuring that Launceston's stories remain as vibrant and haunting as ever.

CHAPTER THIRTEEN
THE PHANTOM CHRISTMAS TREE OF THE WHITE HOUSE

The White House, 1850s

The White House, long a symbol of American power and history, holds many stories within its storied walls. Among them, a lesser-known tale emerges from the shadows each December—the legend of the Phantom Christmas Tree, a haunting memory that intertwines the tragic story of President Franklin Pierce and his family's profound grief. It's a narrative that is part folklore, part history, and entirely wrapped in the sorrow of a family torn apart by loss, lingering in the White House long after their time.

Franklin Pierce, the 14th President of the United States, is often credited with introducing the first Christmas tree to the White House in 1856. The tree's presence marked a moment of hope and an attempt at healing in a time of deep personal tragedy for the Pierce family. The tradition, however, was born not out of simple holiday cheer but as a desperate attempt to lift the spirits of Jane Pierce, the First Lady, who was profoundly affected by the death of their youngest son, Benjamin, known as Bennie.

Franklin Pierce, the 14th President of the United States

The tree, adorned with ornaments and decorations, was intended to bring some semblance of holiday joy into the grief-filled halls of the White House. Jane Pierce had lost three children, with Bennie's death being the most recent and traumatic. Bennie, just 11 years old, died in a horrifying train accident in January 1853, only months before Pierce's inauguration. The accident shattered the family, with Jane Pierce withdrawing almost entirely from public life, over-come by grief and convinced that Bennie's death was a divine punishment.

The idea to place a Christmas tree in the White House came as a suggestion from Jane's doctors, hoping it might lift her spirits. Pierce, desperate to find some way to ease his wife's sorrow, agreed to the plan. They invited children from a local Sunday School to gather and sing carols around the tree, hoping that the innocence and joy of the children would bring comfort to Jane.

While the tree itself may have been a new tradition, it was overshadowed by the heavy aura of loss that surrounded the Pierces. Jane, often described as a spectral figure during her time in the White House, roamed the halls in mourning clothes, unable to move past her grief. She wrote letters to her deceased son Bennie, hoping somehow that her words would reach him beyond the grave. Her sense of loss was so profound that she even attempted to reach Bennie through spiritualist practices, including sessions with mediums.

This deep connection to the supernatural and attempts to communicate with the deceased added to the atmosphere of mystery surrounding the White House during their time there. It was not only Jane's sorrow that lingered; some believe it left an imprint so strong that it can still be felt today. The grief of the Pierces, particularly during the Christmas season, became the seed of the story of a ghostly Christmas tree—a spectral symbol of a Christmas past, frozen in time, as if the White House itself had absorbed their pain.

Over the years, stories have circulated about a ghostly Christmas tree appearing in the White House around the holiday season. White House staff, often tasked with decorating for the holidays, have reported eerie occurrences during these times. Some have claimed to see a faintly glowing tree in the shadows of the rooms, particularly near the location where the original 1856 tree was placed. Others have reported hearing the faint sound of children's laughter or carol singing, even when no one else is in the building.

The most chilling accounts describe a figure, sometimes identified as Jane Pierce, moving through the halls, her dark mourning clothes blending with the shadows. Her spectral presence is said to linger near the space where the Christmas tree was first displayed, as if she remains tied to that moment in time—one when she briefly believed she could feel Bennie's presence again.

These tales of the ghostly Christmas tree remain part of the rich tapestry of White House folklore, mingling with other ghost stories like the famous sightings of Abraham Lincoln's spirit. But unlike Lincoln's more prominent ghostly presence, the Phantom Christmas Tree is shrouded in melancholy, a memory of a family's sorrow that resurfaces during a season traditionally meant for joy.

Franklin and Jane Pierce's time in the White House was marred by their personal tragedy, and the memory of Bennie's death haunted them throughout Franklin's presidency. Jane's depression deepened over the years, with her mourning attire and withdrawn nature becoming a subject of concern for those close to the administration. Although the Christmas tree brought a brief moment of light, it could not lift the persistent shadow cast by their loss.

After leaving the White House, the Pierce family's suffering continued. Jane died in 1863, her spirit broken by years of grief. Franklin Pierce himself succumbed to heavy drinking and died in 1869, his health deteriorated by years of sorrow and guilt over the tragedies that had befallen his family. But the memory of their anguish, it seems, remained tied to the White House, contributing to its reputation as one of the most haunted buildings in America.

The story of the Phantom Christmas Tree of the White House serves as a haunting reminder of the intersection between history and folklore. It embodies the way in which grief, loss, and hope can imprint themselves onto a place, leaving echoes that resonate through time. Franklin Pierce's introduction of the Christmas tree to the White House, while a significant cultural moment, became intertwined with a narrative of mourning, giving rise to the legend of a ghostly holiday tradition that reappears each December.

To this day, the White House remains a place where the past lingers close to the surface, particularly during the holiday season when the halls are dressed in festive splendor. And for those who know the story of the Pierces, there is a sense that beneath the garlands and twinkling lights lies a memory of that first Christmas tree—a tree that might still glow faintly in the shadows, a ghostly beacon for a family's enduring sorrow.

The White House, with its long history, has always been a magnet for tales of the supernatural. The legend of the Phantom Christmas Tree fits well within the broader history of hauntings that include reports of Abraham Lincoln pacing the halls, the disembodied footsteps of past residents, and the sounds of laughter or weeping in the night. Yet, the story of Franklin Pierce, Jane, and the tree is unique in its poignancy. It captures not only the spectral elements that so many ghost stories thrive on but also a deeply human story of a family shattered by tragedy, trying to find a glimmer of hope amid their sorrow.

Today, the tale of the Phantom Christmas Tree is often overshadowed by other, more sensational ghost stories associated with the White House. But for those who cherish the more subtle, melancholic threads of history, it remains a powerful reminder that even in a place as grand as the White House, the echoes of personal heartbreak can linger long after the lights have dimmed. The holiday season, a time of both joy and reflection, becomes the perfect moment for these echoes to reemerge, reminding all who hear them that even the grandest of places have shadows where the past is never truly gone.

CHAPTER FOURTEEN
THE GHOST OF CHRISTMAS PAST AT ALCATRAZ

Alcatraz Prison in San Francisco Bay

Alcatraz Island, a bleak and isolated rock in the middle of San Francisco Bay, is famous for its unforgiving history as a maximum-security prison. Beyond the tales of notorious inmates like Al Capone and Robert Stroud, the "Birdman of Alcatraz," the island has earned a reputation for ghostly occurrences and unexplained phenomena. Among the most enduring and unsettling legends is that of a mysterious woman's sobbing, heard around Christmas time. This chapter explores the haunting story of the Christmas ghost of Alcatraz, blending the history of the island with eerie testimonies and spectral lore that have fascinated visitors and ghost hunters alike.

Before becoming a federal penitentiary in 1934, Alcatraz served multiple purposes, from a military fortification to a military prison. Its origins date back to the 19th century, and over the years, the island bore witness to numerous deaths, including those from failed escape attempts, suicides, and violent altercations among prisoners. The very nature of the island—isolated, cold, and surrounded by the treacherous waters of the bay—has always lent itself to tales of haunt-ings. Native Americans long considered the site a place of malevolent spirits, a sentiment that persisted throughout its history.

The transition to a federal prison only amplified Alcatraz's ominous aura. Known as "The Rock," it was home to some of the country's most hardened criminals, confined under conditions meant to break their spirits. The infamous D-Block, especially the solitary cells known as "The Hole," became a focal point for many ghost stories. Yet, amid the accounts of spectral prisoners, one story stands out for its oddity: the sound of a woman weeping, despite there never having been any female prisoners housed on the island.

The ghostly sobbing is most frequently associated with the ruins of the warden's house. Positioned near the main prison block, the house once hosted the families of Alcatraz wardens, offering a stark contrast between the domestic life of children and spouses and the grim reality of the incarcerated just steps away. Today, the house is in ruins, abandoned to the elements and time, but its derelict remains are a focal point for paranormal enthusiasts.

The legend of the woman's sobbing is particularly tied to the holiday season. Former guards and park rangers have reported hearing the sounds of a woman crying around Christmas time, often near the warden's house or on the path leading from it to the main cell blocks. The sobs are described as soft yet persistent, cutting through the cold air and fog that frequently envelops the island during winter. These sounds, while faint, are said to evoke a profound sense of sadness and loss, leaving those who hear them with chills.

One of the earliest documented encounters occurred in the 1940s, when Warden James A. Johnston, known for his no-nonsense approach, allegedly heard the sobbing while giving a tour to guests. He brushed it off initially, but when his guests mentioned hearing the same mournful sounds, he was unable to provide an explanation. Despite the logical mind of a lawman, even Johnston found himself at a loss when confronted with the inexplicable.

The mystery of the sobbing woman is puzzling because there are no records of any women dying on the island during its time as a prison. Some theories suggest that the spirit could predate the prison era, perhaps a remnant from Alcatraz's time as a military fort. It's possible that the ghost could be that of a woman mourning a lost loved one—a soldier, or maybe one of the civilian workers who lived on the island during its early days. This theory is supported by the island's long history of fatal accidents and drownings during the 19th century, when the treacherous waters around Alcatraz often claimed lives.

Another possibility is that the ghostly presence is not tied to a specific death but is instead a manifestation of the cumulative sorrow and despair that pervaded the island for so many decades. The prison was a place where hope withered, especially during the holidays, when the isolation felt even more acute. Many inmates would have reflected on the families and lives they left behind, and the contrast between the festive celebrations of the mainland and the grim reality of their own confinement could have fueled a collective anguish that echoes still.

Even after the prison's closure in 1963 and its transformation into a tourist site under the management of the National Park Service, reports of the sobbing woman persisted. Park rangers and night security personnel have recounted their own eerie experiences during quiet December nights. Some have reported hearing faint cries while conducting rounds near the warden's house, accompanied by a sudden drop in temperature, even on otherwise mild nights.

One particularly chilling account came from a ranger in the 1980s, who claimed to hear not only the sobs but also what sounded like whispering voices that grew louder the closer he got to the ruins of the warden's house. When he attempted to investigate, he found nothing but the wind howling through the broken windows and crumbling walls. Despite his logical nature, the experience left a deep impression on him, reinforcing the island's reputation as a place where the boundary between the living and the dead is unnervingly thin.

Some visitors have also reported their own unsettling experiences, particularly those who join the nighttime tours that are offered on the island. These tours, which delve into the darker history of Alcatraz, have become a popular draw for those interested in paranormal activity. On occasion, tourists claim to hear the same inexplicable sobbing while exploring the grounds. These encounters often prompt visitors to question the official history of the island, suggesting that there may be more to Alcatraz's haunted past than is recorded in the archives.

The haunting tale of the woman's sobbing at Christmas resonates deeply with the themes of loss and isolation that are central to the history of Alcatraz. For the prisoners who spent their holidays on The Rock, Christmas was a reminder of the life they had forfeited. The Christmas ghost embodies this sense of longing, an enduring presence that continues to evoke the pain of those who once resided on the island, both as prisoners and as family members of the guards.

As winter fog rolls over the island and the lights of San Francisco twinkle in the distance, the ghostly sobs carry a poignant reminder of the emotional toll that Alcatraz exacted on all who lived and worked there. The sobbing woman, whether a real spirit or a collective hallucination born of loneliness, symbolizes the lingering sorrow of a place that was designed to strip away the human spirit. Each December, as tourists explore the desolate remnants of the prison, they might just catch a glimpse—or a sound—of Alcatraz's Christmas ghost, a spectral visitor from the past, eternally mourning through the cold, dark nights.

The legend of the sobbing woman at Alcatraz is more than just a ghost story; it is a reflection of the island's complex and tragic history. It captures the enduring fascination with a place that once held some of America's most infamous criminals, yet it also reminds us that the echoes of human emotion—grief, regret, and longing—can transcend time. Whether the sobbing is the voice of a spirit or the echo of a thousand lonely Christmases, the story of Alcatraz's Christmas ghost ensures that the island remains a place where history and the supernatural intertwine, luring those curious enough to seek its hidden mysteries.

CHAPTER FIFTEEN
THE GHOSTLY CHRISTMAS CARD

Violet Jessop, known as "Miss Unsinkable"

Violet Jessop, known as "Miss Unsinkable" due to her remarkable survival of three major ship disasters—the *Titanic, Britannic,* and a serious incident aboard the *Olympic* —led a life filled with extraordinary experiences. Despite the challenges she faced at sea, Jessop's post-war life took a turn towards quieter and more mysterious encounters, including a story involving a peculiar Christmas card.

After surviving the sinking of both the *Titanic* in 1912 and the *Britannic* in 1916 during World War I, Violet Jessop resumed her life at sea, eventually retiring in 1950. By then, she had endured some of the 20th century's most harrowing maritime disasters. Her life, however, continued to attract intrigue long after she left the sea. Among the many stories circulating about her, one particularly eerie tale involves a Christmas card she received in the 1920s, allegedly from her deceased brother.

Jessop's brother had died in World War I, which deeply affected her, as their family was closely knit. Several years after his death, around 1920, Jessop claimed she received a Christmas card that bore his unmistakable handwriting. This card arrived mysteriously, with no return address or any clue as to how it could have been sent. Given the close resemblance of the handwriting to her brother's, Jessop was perplexed and unsettled by this event. She could find no logical explanation for the card's origin, leading to speculation about paranormal phenomena and messages from beyond the grave.

While some biographical accounts of Violet Jessop focus mainly on her maritime survivals, the tale of the ghostly Christmas card illustrates the enigmatic aspects of her later life. This story, though not as well-documented as her more famous exploits, adds a layer of mystery to the life of a woman already surrounded by tales of resilience and uncanny fortune.

Jessop's story resonates as a mix of tragedy, fortitude, and inexplicable events, making her a compelling figure in historical narratives. Even after enduring the terrors of the ocean, she faced mysteries that were harder to explain than the perils of the sea.

CHAPTER SIXTEEN
THE CHRISTMAS TRAIN HAUNTINGS

Illustration of the bridge collapse

The holiday season is often associated with joy and celebration, but in some corners of the world, it's also a time when the veil between the living and the dead feels thinner. Among the stories of ghostly apparitions tied to Christmas time, the legend of the Ashtabula train disaster stands out as a chilling reminder of the past. On a snowy Christmas Eve in 1876, a tragic event unfolded in Ashtabula, Ohio, that continues to echo through time. The stories of a ghostly train, phantom whistles, and the apparitions of those lost that night have become part of the area's folklore. This chapter delves into the history of the Ashtabula train wreck, the subsequent hauntings, and the enduring mystery surrounding this eerie event.

On December 29, 1876, just days after Christmas, the town of Ashtabula, Ohio, witnessed one of the most catastrophic train disasters in American history. The Pacific Express, a luxury train operated by the Lake Shore and Michigan Southern Railway, was en route from Erie, Pennsylvania, to Chicago. Despite being built with the best engineering of the time, the bridge that spanned the Ashtabula River collapsed under the weight of the train during a blizzard, sending cars plunging into the icy waters below.

The disaster was immediate and horrific. Approximately 160 passengers were on board, and the initial collapse killed many. But the real horror came when the train's stoves and lamps ignited a fire among the wreckage, burning those who survived the initial fall. The intense cold and the treacherous conditions hampered rescue efforts, and by the next morning, only charred remains of the cars and their occupants remained. Of the 92 who perished, only 47 were ever identified, leaving many families without closure as the remains of their loved ones were never recovered.

The tragedy left a deep scar on the community, but it also gave rise to unsettling tales of hauntings and spectral apparitions that continue to haunt the town of Ashtabula and its surrounding areas.

The Ashtabula disaster is not just a story of structural failure and tragic loss; it has also become a part of the supernatural lore of the region. Locals and visitors alike have reported eerie occurrences near the site of the disaster, especially around the Christmas season. Tales of ghostly train sounds —phantom whistles, the clacking of wheels on long-rusted tracks, and even the distant screams of passengers—are often shared among the residents of Ashtabula. Many believe that the spirits of those who died in the wreck continue to roam the area, seeking rest that they never found in life.

One of the most reported apparitions is that of a spectral train moving through the night along the route that once connected the Ashtabula station to the ill-fated bridge. Witnesses claim to see the dim glow of a locomotive's light cutting through the dark winter fog, only for it to vanish suddenly, leaving behind a chilling silence. Some have described seeing shadowy figures walking near the Ashtabula River or along the snow-covered tracks, figures that disappear upon approach.

The town's Chestnut Grove Cemetery, where many of the unidentified victims were interred, is another hotspot for paranormal activity. Visitors to the cemetery during the Christmas season have reported seeing misty apparitions and hearing faint cries on cold winter nights. Some say they feel an inexplicable chill in the air and hear whispers among the gravestones, as if the spirits are trying to convey a message from beyond the grave.

The stories of the haunted train and its spectral passengers have persisted for over a century, but explanations for these phenomena vary. Some paranormal researchers suggest that the intensity of the disaster, with its sudden and violent nature, left a kind of "psychic imprint" on the area. The abrupt end to so many lives, especially during the holidays, is believed to have created a lingering energy that replays the tragedy like a loop on the anniversary of the disaster.

Skeptics, however, attribute the sightings to a mix of natural sounds and the power of local legend. The area around the Ashtabula River is known for its peculiar acoustics, especially when the wind sweeps through the valley. These natural sounds, coupled with the already chilling story of the train wreck, might explain why people believe they hear the whistle of a ghost train or the cries of the deceased. Yet, even these rational explanations fail to account for the numerous reports of spectral figures and the consistent timing of these apparitions around Christmas.

The legacy of the Ashtabula train disaster extends beyond tales of ghostly sightings; it has left a profound mark on the town's culture and history. The tragedy led to a major investigation into railroad safety standards and the structural soundness of bridges, influencing changes across the industry. But despite these advances, the disaster's human toll continues to resonate most deeply with those who live in and around Ashtabula.

In the decades that followed the disaster, the town erected memorials and held services to remember the lives lost that fateful night. Chestnut Grove Cemetery, where many of the unidentified victims are buried, remains a place of reflection and solemn remembrance. It is not uncommon for locals to visit the graves during the holiday season, leaving flowers or lighting candles in honor of the dead. Many feel a connection to those lost in the disaster, seeing them as part of the town's collective memory, forever intertwined with the story of Ashtabula.

While some stories of the ghost train have been passed down through generations, contemporary accounts continue to emerge. Ghost hunters, paranormal enthusiasts, and curious visitors have taken to exploring the ruins of the old tracks and the surrounding woods, hoping to catch a glimpse of the phantom train. Some have claimed to capture ghostly voices on recording devices, while others report feeling a sense of overwhelming sadness or dread when visiting the site. These accounts are frequently shared on online forums and paranormal investigation websites, adding new layers to the ongoing legend of the Ashtabula train hauntings.

Local businesses have also embraced the haunted history of the area, organizing ghost tours that lead participants through the key locations connected to the disaster. These tours have become popular during the holiday season, offering a darker twist to the usual Christmas festivities. Some see these tours as a way to keep the memory of the disaster alive, while others hope to find proof of the supernatural amid the echoes of the past.

The story of the Ashtabula train disaster of 1876 is a poignant reminder of how closely the past can cling to the present. The tragedy that unfolded in a snowy Ohio town has left behind more than just a legacy of loss; it has given rise to tales of hauntings that blur the lines between history and legend. For some, these ghostly encounters serve as a way to remember and honor those who perished, while for others, they are a source of fascination and mystery. As the snow falls over Ashtabula each December, the whispers of a phantom train and the shadows along the river remind all who listen that some stories, like the spirits of Christmas past, never truly fade away.

CHAPTER SEVENTEEN
THE GHOST OF SIR GEORGE VILLIERS

George Villiers portrait

One of the most unsettling Christmas ghost stories in English history is that of Sir George Villiers, whose spirit supposedly appeared to warn of impending tragedy. Sir George Villiers, the father of George Villiers, the first Duke of

Buckingham, died in 1606, long before his son's fateful assassination in 1628. Yet, according to several accounts, his ghost appeared to warn of his son's imminent demise. This tale of spectral visitation, tied closely to Christmas and the spirit's appearance during the winter months, has become a chilling story of a ghostly message that went unheeded, leading to a tragic outcome. The story not only explores the supernatural but also hints at the complex intertwining of fate, warnings, and the political turbulence of 17th-century England.

George Villiers, the first Duke of Buckingham, was a prominent figure in the court of King James I and later King Charles I, known for his influence and ambition. His father, Sir George Villiers, was less politically influential but played a key role in the narrative of his son's demise through the spectral visitations attributed to him. Sir George's ghost was reported to have appeared to a former acquaintance named John Towes. Towes was described as a former servant or close associate of the Villiers family, someone who would have been familiar with Sir George in life. The apparition reportedly instructed Towes to warn the Duke of Buckingham about his dangerous behavior and the risks he faced in his political role.

The ghostly figure was described vividly, wearing clothes that Sir George might have worn in life, making it immediately recognizable to Towes. According to some versions, the spirit revealed secret signs or intimate knowledge that only Sir George or someone close to him could have known. This specificity was intended to convince Towes of the seriousness and authenticity of the message. However, when Towes relayed the warnings to the Duke of Buckingham, he was met with skepticism. The Duke dismissed the tales as mere superstition, despite the eerie nature of the warnings.

Sir George's ghost, according to some accounts, did not appear just once but repeatedly, each time urging Towes to deliver his dire message. The urgency of the spirit's appearance increased, eventually including a specific prediction: that the Duke would be stabbed if he did not take heed of the warning. The prophecy was chillingly accurate. On August 23, 1628, George Villiers, the Duke of Buckingham, was assassinated by John Felton, a disgruntled soldier, in Portsmouth. The details of this assassination, including its violent and sudden nature, aligned closely with the warnings provided by the apparition.

This tragic outcome lent an air of credibility to the tale of Sir George's ghost, turning it from a mere story of spectral appearances into one of prophecy and fate. The notion that a spirit could return from beyond the grave with such precision to warn of mortal danger adds a layer of supernatural intrigue to the historical narrative. It has been suggested that this spectral intervention was not merely a family ghost story but part of a broader tradition of apparitions that serve as omens in British folklore.

To understand why this story became so significant, it is essential to consider the context of early 17th-century England. George Villiers was not just a powerful nobleman; he was a highly controversial figure. As a close confidant of King James I, and later King Charles I, he wielded considerable power, which earned him many enemies at court. His influence, often perceived as overreach, made him a target for public and political animosity. This animosity ultimately created the conditions for his assassination by John Felton, who believed that the Duke was responsible for many of England's troubles at the time.

The story of Sir George's ghostly warning is deeply intertwined with this historical moment. In a time when omens and supernatural occurrences were often believed to carry great significance, the tale of a ghost forewarning a murder would have resonated powerfully. Moreover, Christmas, with its associations with both festive joy and eerie winter nights, provided a fitting backdrop for the spectral tale. Ghost stories were a popular part of Christmas traditions during this period, often told during long winter evenings by the fire. The timing of Sir George's spectral appearances, around the Christmas season, added an extra layer of dread and melancholy to the story.

While the warning to the Duke of Buckingham is the most famous of Sir George Villiers's spectral appearances, it is not the only instance where his ghost is said to have manifested. Over the centuries, various stories have emerged of his apparition being seen in places like Windsor Castle, a site long associated with ghostly tales of British royalty. The ghost's appearance is often described as a harbinger of ill fortune, fitting into a broader tradition of ghostly warnings in British lore.

Such stories have been recorded and retold by antiquarians and ghost story enthusiasts, contributing to the enduring nature of the tale. For example, the story was mentioned in the writings of John Aubrey, a 17th-century antiquary known for collecting tales of the supernatural. Aubrey's accounts suggest that the ghost of Sir George appeared several times to those connected to the Villiers family, each time bringing warnings or attempting to convey some message from the afterlife.

The story of Sir George Villiers's ghost has all the hallmarks of a classic tragic narrative: a dire warning, a fateful prophecy, and a tragic hero who ultimately ignores the signs meant to save him. In the end, the Duke's assassination was seen by some as an inevitable outcome, foretold by a spirit from beyond the grave. This narrative fits well within the cultural landscape of the time, where the supernatural was often seen as interwoven with the everyday and where ghostly apparitions were taken as serious omens.

The spectral warning of Sir George also serves as a reminder of the fragility of power and the uncertainty of human life. Even a figure as influential as the Duke of Buckingham was not immune to the mysterious forces of fate. His story, alongside the chilling tales of his father's ghost, continues to capture the imagination of those who encounter it. Each retelling brings the shadowy figure of Sir George back to life, a reminder that some messages from the past linger on, refusing to be forgotten.

The tale of Sir George Villiers and his ghostly warnings has endured through the centuries, a story passed down through the layers of English history and folklore. It serves as both a cautionary tale and a reflection of the beliefs and anxieties of its time. The spectral warnings, given and ignored, create a narrative rich with themes of regret, destiny, and the unending attempts to alter the course of events—even from beyond the grave.

To this day, the story remains a fascinating example of how ghost stories have been used to make sense of tragic events and unexplained phenomena. Whether viewed as a true account of spectral intervention or as a product of a society deeply attuned to the supernatural, the haunting of Sir George Villiers adds a touch of eerie mystery to the winter nights, where tales of ghosts are still told in the shadows of flickering candlelight. As the holiday season approaches, the story of Sir George's ghost serves as a reminder of the darker side of Christmas, where ghosts linger not only in memory but perhaps in the very air, seeking to be heard.

CHAPTER EIGHTEEN
THE DISAPPEARING CHRISTMAS TREE OF HOUSE OF FRASER

The story of the disappearing Christmas tree at the House of Fraser department store in Edinburgh is a haunting tale that captures the imagination, blending elements of the supernatural with the city's rich history of ghostly folklore. Set in the 1970s, this curious event became a topic of fascination and mystery for locals and visitors alike, adding to Edinburgh's reputation as one of the most haunted cities in the world.

The House of Fraser, a well-known department store chain, has long been a part of Edinburgh's retail landscape. Located on Princes Street, the building itself is historic, with a structure dating back to the 19th century. It was an integral part of Edinburgh's shopping experience, especially during the holiday season, when it transformed into a winter wonderland, complete with elaborate decorations and Christmas displays that drew families from across the city.

The incident of the disappearing Christmas tree is said to have occurred during one particularly cold winter in the 1970s. The store had put up a large, beautifully decorated tree, adorned with twinkling lights and traditional ornaments. This centerpiece was meant to evoke the holiday spirit among shoppers, but instead, it became the center of a chilling mystery.

According to reports from employees working late one evening, the tree seemed to vanish before their eyes. One moment, it was standing in the middle of the store's display area; the next, it was simply gone, leaving only an eerie silence. Witnesses claimed that strange noises accompanied the event, including whispers, the sound of distant footsteps, and even faint bells that seemed to come from nowhere.

The sudden disappearance of the tree sparked a wave of speculation and rumors. Some employees believed that the store was haunted, a theory that seemed plausible given Edinburgh's reputation for ghost stories and paranormal activities. Edinburgh, known for its haunted alleys, cemeteries, and ancient buildings, has always had a dark side. Tales of spirits wandering the Old Town or eerie happenings at famous sites like Greyfriars Kirkyard have been common. Thus, the House of Fraser incident quickly became part of this lore.

Other staff members speculated that a prankster might have been behind the tree's disappearance, but no evidence ever emerged to support this idea. The absence of any signs of a break-in or theft made the event even more perplexing. Security footage from the time was inconclusive, adding to the sense of mystery. As time went on, the incident evolved from a strange occurrence into a local legend.

Paranormal enthusiasts who delved into the mystery of the disappearing tree suggested that the building's history might hold clues. Before becoming part of the House of Fraser chain, the store had been known by other names and served different purposes over the decades. Some claimed that the ghost of a former worker or a restless spirit from the past might have caused the disturbance, seeking to make its presence known during the Christmas season.

Edinburgh's long history of ghost sightings added credibility to these theories. The city has always been a magnet for ghost hunters and those interested in the supernatural. Haunted tours often point out locations such as the infamous vaults beneath the city, where spirits are said to linger. For those who believed in such things, the incident at the House of Fraser seemed like a continuation of Edinburgh's eerie traditions.

After the tree's disappearance, some employees reported feeling a chill in the air during night shifts, or claimed to have seen shadowy figures out of the corner of their eyes.

Others dismissed these accounts as mere imagination, fueled by the unsettling events that winter. The story of the vanishing tree spread by word of mouth, turning it into a popular tale among locals and visitors interested in the city's supernatural side.

While the House of Fraser incident never led to any formal investigation or public statements from the store, it has remained a part of Edinburgh's haunted folklore. It is often mentioned alongside other ghost stories from the city, such as the poltergeist of the South Bridge vaults or the apparitions seen at Edinburgh Castle. The story serves as a reminder of the ways in which history, mystery, and folklore blend in Edinburgh's unique cultural landscape.

The story of the disappearing Christmas tree endures not just because of its supernatural elements but because it captures a moment in time when the line between the ordinary and the extraordinary seemed to blur. It taps into the timeless appeal of ghost stories, particularly those set during the Christmas season—a time when tales of the otherworldly have long held a special place in the imagination, from Charles Dickens' *A Christmas Carol* to local legends whispered around the fireplace.

In the years since, Edinburgh has continued to attract those fascinated by the paranormal. Ghost tours, books, and documentaries often revisit tales like that of the House of Fraser, exploring them as part of the city's rich tapestry of folklore. The mystery of the disappearing Christmas tree, with its unanswered questions and chilling atmosphere, remains a vivid chapter in Edinburgh's long history of hauntings.

CHAPTER NINETEEN
THE GHOSTS OF THE HOTEL DEL CORONADO

Hotel Del Coronado

San Diego's Hotel Del Coronado is a storied resort, known not only for its historic architecture and stunning ocean views but also for being home to one of the most enduring ghost stories in California. The tale centers around Kate Morgan, a young woman whose death in 1892 has left a lingering presence that many believe still haunts the hotel to this day.

Kate Morgan checked into the hotel on Thanksgiving Day, November 24, 1892, under the pseudonym "Mrs. Lottie A. Bernard" from Detroit. Described by the hotel staff as beautiful yet troubled, she seemed to carry a mysterious sadness. According to accounts, Kate told various stories during her brief stay, ranging from waiting for her brother—a doctor— to claiming that she suffered from a serious illness. None of these stories matched up, adding an air of intrigue to her stay.

Kate Morgan

Five days after checking in, Kate was found dead on an exterior staircase leading to the beach, with a gunshot wound to her head. A handgun, purchased in San Diego during her stay, was found near her body. The official ruling was suicide, but the circumstances surrounding her death have remained controversial. Some believe that the caliber of the bullet did not match her gun, suggesting the possibility of foul play. However, the case was never reopened, and the mystery of Kate's last days endures.

Since her death, many guests and staff members have reported encountering what they believe to be the restless spirit of Kate Morgan. Her former room—now numbered 3327, though it was room 302 during her stay—has become a focal point for ghostly experiences. Visitors to the room often speak of unexplained phenomena, such as flickering lights, sudden chills, and objects moving of their own accord. The television reportedly turns on and off by itself, and some guests have even claimed to hear whispers and footsteps when no one else is present.

The stories don't end with her room. Throughout the hotel, particularly in the gift shop, eerie occurrences are frequently reported. Items are said to fly off the shelves, but they land gently without breaking. It's these peculiar and seemingly playful incidents that have convinced many that Kate's spirit remains active in the hotel. Paranormal investigators have even spent nights in room 3327, armed with high-tech equipment to document these strange happenings, further cementing its reputation as a haunted hotspot.

Despite the intrigue surrounding her death, much of Kate Morgan's life remains shrouded in mystery. Born around 1864 in Iowa, she lived a life marked by tragedy and instability. After her mother's death, she was raised by her grandfather. She later married Thomas Edwin Morgan, but their marriage was troubled, particularly after the death of their infant son. The marriage eventually ended, and Kate reportedly began a series of transient relationships and travels across the country.

When she arrived at the Hotel Del Coronado, Kate seemed to be running from her past, but what exactly she sought remains unknown. Some speculate she hoped to reunite with a lover who never showed up, leaving her alone and desperate. Others think she sought a peaceful place to end her life, having faced so much sorrow. Her death, steeped in ambiguity, has led to widespread speculation and a lasting fascination that has endured for more than a century.

Room 3327 today.

Today, the Hotel Del Coronado embraces its haunted history, offering tours that delve into the mystery of Kate Morgan and the other spirits said to linger on the premises. Room 3327 remains the most requested room in the hotel, with thrill-seekers hoping for a brush with the supernatural.

Guests have recounted stories of waking up to a cold breeze, even when the windows are tightly closed, and finding their belongings mysteriously rearranged.

Beyond her room, the hotel's grand Victorian halls, elegant Crown Room, and beachfront have all been sites of supposed encounters with Kate's ghostly figure. She has been seen wandering the shore, perhaps searching for the peace that eluded her in life. The hotel's gift shop, too, remains a hub of paranormal activity, with staff and visitors reporting inexplicable disturbances.

The question of whether Kate's death was truly a suicide or something more sinister has kept amateur sleuths and historians intrigued for decades. The theory of foul play gained traction when a San Francisco lawyer named Alan May revisited the case in the 1980s. May noted inconsistencies in the coroner's report, suggesting that the bullet found in Kate's head did not match the caliber of her gun. Although this theory brought new attention to the case, it failed to produce concrete evidence and the case was never officially reopened.

Others believe that Kate's own turmoil led her to take her life, with the quiet beach and the grandeur of the hotel providing a final, tragic setting. Her actions in the days leading up to her death—buying a gun, isolating herself, and expressing despair—have been seen as signs of a troubled state of mind.

For many, the allure of the Hotel Del Coronado goes beyond its beautiful architecture and oceanfront views. It's the promise of a ghostly encounter that brings countless visitors each year, hoping for a glimpse into the past or a brush with the unexplained. The story of Kate Morgan is more than just a ghost story; it's a narrative woven with themes of love, loss, and the mysteries that linger when a life is cut short.

The fascination with Kate's story has become an integral part of the hotel's identity, blending history with legend. While skeptics may dismiss the sightings and strange occurrences as overactive imaginations or the quirks of an old building, the tales continue to draw curiosity. Paranormal enthusiasts and casual visitors alike are drawn to room 3327, the hotel's shadowy hallways, and the windswept beach where Kate's story came to its sorrowful end.

The story of Kate Morgan and the Hotel Del Coronado is a testament to the enduring power of mystery and the human fascination with the unknown. More than 130 years after her death, Kate's spirit, real or imagined, continues to walk the halls of the historic hotel, leaving behind a legacy of whispers and chills. The legend of Kate Morgan offers a reminder that some stories, like her restless spirit, never truly fade away—they linger, echoing through time, like the sound of waves crashing against the Coronado shore.

Whether you believe in ghosts or not, the tale of Kate Morgan serves as a compelling chapter in the history of the Hotel Del Coronado. It invites us to ponder the mysteries that lie beyond our understanding and to explore the shadows where history and folklore intertwine.

CHAPTER TWENTY

THE CHRISTMAS EVE APPARITION AT HAMPTON COURT PALACE

Hampton Court Palace

Hampton Court Palace, a sprawling Tudor estate on the banks of the River Thames, is not only renowned for its architectural grandeur and royal history but also for its haunted reputation. Among the palace's most infamous ghost stories is the tale of Catherine Howard, the fifth wife of

Henry VIII. Her spectral presence is said to haunt the "Haunted Gallery" at Hampton Court, where, according to legend, she desperately ran and screamed for mercy on the eve of her execution. This chapter delves into the story of Catherine Howard, the chilling events leading up to her death, and the eerie encounters reported by visitors to the palace—particularly on Christmas Eve, when her ghost is said to be most active.

Catherine Howard portrait

Catherine Howard's life was marked by a rapid rise to power and an equally swift and tragic downfall. Born around 1523, Catherine was a cousin of Anne Boleyn, Henry VIII's second wife. She grew up in the household of her step-grandmother, the Dowager Duchess of Norfolk, where discipline was lax, and she was exposed to romantic liaisons from an early age.

When she entered the court as a lady-in-waiting to Henry's fourth wife, Anne of Cleves, Catherine caught the eye of the aging king. Her youth and beauty captivated Henry, and after the annulment of his marriage to Anne, he married Catherine in 1540.

Catherine's marriage to Henry was fraught with challenges. Despite being queen, she engaged in an affair with Thomas Culpeper, a courtier, which would prove to be her undoing. As rumors of her past indiscretions and present infidelities reached the king, Henry's affection turned to fury. By November 1541, he had ordered her arrest.

Catherine Howard's arrest at Hampton Court Palace is the centerpiece of the haunting legend. After learning of her impending charges, she is said to have escaped her guards and raced down the long gallery that now bears the name "Haunted Gallery," screaming and begging for the king's mercy. Henry VIII was reportedly praying in the nearby Chapel Royal at the time, but Catherine's cries went unanswered. Guards quickly apprehended her and dragged her back to her chambers.

Her desperate flight through the gallery has been a source of fascination and terror for centuries. According to accounts, the young queen's panicked footsteps and anguished cries can still be heard echoing through the corridors on certain nights, particularly around Christmas. This seasonal connection has been a point of intrigue, with the story gaining traction as a Christmas Eve haunting, when visitors claim the atmosphere becomes especially eerie.

Christmas Eve at Hampton Court Palace has a unique, unsettling atmosphere. Visitors and staff have often reported strange occurrences in the Haunted Gallery during this time. Some claim to see a pale, spectral figure believed to be Catherine herself, running through the gallery in the same desperate manner she did centuries ago. Witnesses describe a chilling drop in temperature, followed by the sensation of being watched or accompanied by an unseen presence as they walk through the historic passage.

The most vivid reports involve hearing faint but unmistakable screams echoing along the gallery. These wails are said to mimic Catherine's cries for mercy, as she desperately sought Henry's pardon before her arrest. Such occurrences contribute to the enduring belief that the tragic queen has never left Hampton Court, her spirit trapped in a loop of terror and despair.

The Haunted Gallery itself is a significant feature of Hampton Court Palace. This long corridor, adorned with portraits of Tudor monarchs and historical artifacts, stretches from Henry VIII's private apartments to the Chapel Royal. In the 16th century, it served as a processional route where courtiers would accompany the king during religious services. Today, it stands as a testament to the darker side of Tudor history, drawing ghost hunters and history enthusiasts alike.

Visitors walking through the gallery are often struck by a sudden sense of dread or unease, which many attribute to Catherine's restless spirit. Some have reported feeling a cold hand brushing their shoulder or hearing distant footsteps, even when alone in the space. These experiences add to the gallery's ominous reputation, making it a focal point for ghost tours and paranormal investigations.

The Haunted Gallery

The legend of Catherine Howard's ghost has attracted both skeptics and believers over the years. Paranormal investigators have conducted studies in the Haunted Gallery, using modern technology like thermal imaging and EVP (Electronic Voice Phenomena) devices to capture evidence of supernatural activity. While some have reported anomalies —cold spots, strange noises, and unexplainable energy readings—others suggest that the stories are exaggerated, the result of collective imagination fueled by the palace's dramatic history.

Nonetheless, the enduring tales of Catherine's apparition contribute to Hampton Court's allure, blending historical tragedy with the thrill of the supernatural. During special events around Christmas, the palace leans into its spectral reputation, inviting guests to explore the darker stories associated with its halls. For many, the opportunity to experience the Haunted Gallery on Christmas Eve is a highlight, whether they hope to encounter a ghost or simply revel in the eerie atmosphere.

The question remains: why does the legend of Catherine Howard's ghostly appearance peak around Christmas Eve? Some believe it is tied to the heightened emotions and reflections that come with the holiday season—a time when the boundaries between the past and present feel thinner. For Catherine, Christmas might symbolize a lost hope, a moment when she desperately sought clemency from her husband, only to find herself facing the inevitability of her tragic fate.

Others suggest that the association with Christmas Eve is simply a part of Victorian storytelling traditions, which often emphasized ghostly tales during the holiday season. The Victorian era, known for its fascination with ghost stories, helped cement Hampton Court's reputation as a haunted landmark. Publications from that time frequently featured tales of restless spirits wandering historic English estates, and Catherine Howard's story fit the bill perfectly.

The story of the Christmas Eve Apparition at Hampton Court Palace is one that continues to captivate and unsettle. It is a tale rooted in the dramatic fall of a young queen and her desperate, doomed plea for life. Whether one believes in the supernatural or views these stories as remnants of Tudor history brought to life by the imagination, Catherine Howard's ghostly presence is undeniably a part of Hampton Court's identity. For those who walk the Haunted Gallery on a cold December night, the sense of history mingles with the thrill of the unknown, offering a haunting glimpse into the past that lingers just beneath the surface.

As the clock strikes midnight on Christmas Eve, some might listen closely, hoping to catch the faint echo of a tragic queen's cries—an enduring reminder of the dark and turbulent world of Henry VIII's court.

CHAPTER TWENTY-ONE
THE SILENT GHOSTS OF ICELAND'S CHRISTMAS FOLKLORE

Grýla

Icelandic Christmas traditions are far from the typical jolly depictions of Santa Claus and reindeer-drawn sleighs. Instead, the long, dark winter nights of Iceland harbor a blend of mythological figures and eerie tales. Central to these stories are the Yule Lads, their terrifying mother Grýla, and a variety of spectral entities that make the holiday season one of mystery and chills. This chapter delves into these supernatural elements, exploring how the folklore weaves together ancient traditions, spooky myths, and Iceland's unique take on Christmas celebrations.

The Icelandic Yule Lads

The Yule Lads

The Yule Lads, or Jólasveinar, are a group of thirteen brothers who descend from their mountain homes during the thirteen nights leading up to Christmas. Unlike the benevolent Santa Claus, each Yule Lad has a specific mischief they like to perform. Some sneak into homes to lick spoons (Þvörusleikir), steal sausages (Bjúgnakrækir), or peer through windows (Gluggagægir). Traditionally, the Yule Lads were far more sinister than their modern incarnations, which now leave small gifts for well-behaved children. Historically, they were known to harass households, steal food, and frighten children who misbehaved.

The transformation of the Yule Lads from fearsome figures to more playful pranksters reflects broader cultural changes in Icelandic society. In 1746, the government even banned the most terrifying stories about them to prevent scaring children excessively. Nevertheless, the undercurrent of their eerie origins remains, particularly in rural regions where stories of their haunting presence in the dark, snow-covered landscapes persist.

Grýla, the mother of the Yule Lads, is perhaps the most terrifying character in Icelandic Christmas folklore. Legends of Grýla date back to the 13th century, where she is described as a giantess who comes down from her mountain lair to find and consume misbehaving children. Unlike the Yule Lads, who have softened over time, Grýla's portrayal has retained much of its original horror. She is said to have an insatiable appetite, boiling children in a cauldron to make a hearty stew. This grim narrative served as a cautionary tale to encourage good behavior among children during the darkest time of the year.

Grýla's husband, Leppalúði, plays a much less significant role in these tales, often depicted as lazy and ineffectual compared to his fearsome wife. Grýla and her family live in a cave in the mountains, a setting that complements the desolate winter landscapes of Iceland. This isolation and the harshness of their surroundings reinforce the dread she inspires among those who hear her story.

Another fearsome creature that haunts the Icelandic holiday season is the Jólakötturinn, or the Yule Cat. This giant, spectral feline roams the snowy countryside, preying on anyone who is not wearing new clothing on Christmas Eve. Unlike the Yule Lads, who are mischievous rather than outright malevolent, the Yule Cat is a truly menacing figure, devouring those who fail to meet this peculiar condition. The Yule Cat's origins are thought to reflect Icelandic social norms, encouraging people to work hard and finish tasks like knitting and weaving before the end of the year. Those who complete their work receive new clothes as a reward, and those who don't are left vulnerable to the predatory Yule Cat.

Jólakötturinn, or the Yule Cat

This eerie feline's legend plays a dual role in the Christmas season. It is both a cautionary figure and a symbol of Iceland's deep ties to the natural world, embodying the brutal and unforgiving aspects of the winter landscape.

Beyond the well-known figures of the Yule Lads and their monstrous mother, Icelandic Christmas folklore is filled with ghostly entities and supernatural occurrences. Many Icelanders believe that spirits become more active during the long, dark nights of December, particularly around Christmas and New Year's. This belief stems from ancient Norse customs that considered the solstice a time when the boundaries between the living and the dead were thin.

In some rural parts of Iceland, tales are still told of spirits that knock on doors or rattle windows on Christmas Eve, seeking warmth and comfort from the winter cold. These ghostly visitors are said to be the souls of those who died during harsh winters, trapped between the worlds of the living and the dead. Households would light candles and maintain a tidy home to ward off these spirits, blending practical traditions with supernatural fears.

The belief in such spirits ties into older pagan traditions, where respect for the deceased and offerings to ancestors were crucial elements of midwinter rituals. Icelanders today might not actively practice these customs, but the stories endure, adding to the haunted atmosphere that characterizes the Icelandic holiday season.

While the darker aspects of Icelandic Christmas folklore have been softened over the years, the essence of these stories continues to captivate locals and tourists alike. Modern depictions of the Yule Lads, for instance, present them as quirky characters who still maintain their traditional roles but with a lighter touch. Storytelling events, museum exhibits, and public performances bring these tales to life during the holiday season, allowing visitors to experience Iceland's unique blend of cheer and chill.

Grýla and the Yule Cat remain symbols of Iceland's enduring connection to its folklore, reminders that Christmas in Iceland is as much about mystery and shadows as it is about light and celebration. While the festive elements of Christmas—like twinkling lights and gatherings—are important, the stories of these ghostly figures serve as a powerful reminder of the country's cultural heritage, where the supernatural is never far from the surface.

Iceland's Christmas folklore offers a rich tapestry of stories that combine the warmth of holiday traditions with the cold bite of ancient fears. The Yule Lads, Grýla, the Yule Cat, and the lingering spirits of winter create an atmosphere that is both festive and unsettling, inviting people to embrace a different kind of holiday magic. These tales speak to a culture deeply shaped by its environment, where the long darkness of winter is filled with shadows and whispers of the past. As Icelanders celebrate Christmas today, they do so with an understanding that beneath the cheerful festivities lie echoes of a more mysterious, and perhaps more haunting, time.

CHAPTER TWENTY-TWO
THE CHRISTMAS EVE SEANCE

The story of the Christmas Eve séance in Edinburgh fits snugly within the Victorian-era tradition of ghost stories that captivated many during the 19th century. This chapter delves into the tale of a wealthy family who hosted a séance on Christmas Eve, only to encounter a haunting prophecy that seemed to come tragically true just hours later. This narrative is steeped in the historical atmosphere of Victorian spiritualism, where the blending of festive warmth and eerie tales became a hallmark of the season.

The events of this story take place in Edinburgh, Scotland, during the mid-19th century. At this time, the city was a hub of Victorian culture and tradition, with its grand stone buildings and narrow, fog-laden streets creating an atmosphere ripe for ghostly tales. Victorian Edinburgh was known for its fascination with the supernatural. Séances, mediums, and spirit circles were popular among the upper classes, who often gathered to try to connect with the spirit world.

The city's festive season was marked by a deep appreciation for the macabre and the mysterious. While Christmas might seem a time of joy and warmth, it was also a period when ghost stories were a staple of holiday gatherings. This tradition, which predates even Charles Dickens' *A Christmas Carol*, found a perfect home in Scotland, where the long, cold nights seemed to invite spectral visitors.

In the winter of 1847, a wealthy Edinburgh family decided to host a séance on Christmas Eve in their grand home on the outskirts of the city. They were inspired by the popular Victorian pastime of sharing ghostly tales and the belief that spirits roamed more freely during the cold, dark nights of winter. The house itself, a large stone manor surrounded by snow-covered grounds, had an imposing presence that added to the supernatural ambiance of the night.

The séance was led by a visiting medium, known for her ability to commune with spirits. As the family and a few close friends gathered in a dimly lit parlor, the air was thick with anticipation. They arranged themselves around a table, candles flickering as the medium began to chant softly, invoking the presence of any spirits who might wish to communicate. It is said that the temperature in the room dropped sharply, and a chill seemed to seep into their very bones.

After several minutes of silence, the medium's voice changed, taking on a deeper, almost inhuman tone. Her eyes fluttered shut, and her body tensed as if channeling a powerful presence. Those present would later claim that a cold wind swirled through the room, extinguishing one of the candles. The spirit, speaking through the medium, delivered a dire warning: "Beware the flames, for they come before the dawn."

The family, initially unnerved, tried to dismiss the message as a figment of the medium's imagination or a theatrical flair. However, a sense of unease lingered as the night wore on. Some guests reported feeling a strange pressure in their chests, a sense that they were not alone in the room, even after the séance had ended.

Only hours after the séance, in the early hours of Christmas morning, disaster struck. The family awoke to the acrid smell of smoke and the terrifying sight of flames consuming the lower floors of their home. Despite their efforts to escape, the fire spread rapidly, engulfing the old wooden beams and furnishings. The cause of the fire was never determined—some believed it was an accident, while others whispered of a malevolent spirit's hand in the tragedy.

The fire claimed the lives of several family members, including the medium who had warned them of impending doom. By the time help arrived, much of the house had collapsed, leaving a smoldering ruin where a grand home had once stood. The few survivors were left to grapple with the haunting memory of the spirit's warning, forever linking that Christmas Eve to a tragedy that would not be easily forgotten.

In the years that followed, the burned-out shell of the mansion became a local landmark, a place that many considered cursed. Residents of Edinburgh began to report strange occurrences near the ruins, particularly around Christmastime. Some claimed to see a shadowy figure moving among the rubble, a dark silhouette that appeared and vanished without a trace. It was said that this figure moved with an otherworldly grace, gliding through the snow-covered grounds as if searching for something—or someone.

Witnesses described the figure as wearing old-fashioned clothing, with a cloak that billowed in the wind, even on calm nights. The apparition's face was always obscured by shadow, adding to the mystery. Those brave enough to venture near the ruins on Christmas Eve reported hearing faint whispers carried on the wind, as if the spirits trapped in the fire were still trying to warn the living of dangers yet to come.

The tale of the Christmas Eve séance and the tragic fire that followed became a part of Edinburgh's rich tapestry of ghost stories. For many, it served as a reminder of the power of the unseen and the thin veil between the living and the dead, especially during the darkest nights of the year. The ruins of the manor, overgrown with ivy and half-buried under decades of snow and decay, became a site for curious visitors and paranormal enthusiasts alike.

Local lore holds that on cold, snowy nights around Christmas, one can still hear the crackle of ghostly flames in the distance, mingled with the faint cries of those lost in the fire. Some claim that if you stand quietly near the ruins on Christmas Eve, you can feel a chill that cuts to the bone, a coldness that is more than just the winter air.

The story of the Christmas Eve séance in 19th-century Edinburgh captures the essence of Victorian fascination with the supernatural. It intertwines the warmth of holiday traditions with the chilling presence of spirits, a combination that made Christmas a time not just for joy and celebration, but also for ghostly tales that whispered of life beyond death. In a city where history and legend often overlap, the tale of the shadowy figure at the ruins remains a testament to the enduring allure of the unknown, even in the heart of the festive season.

This legend, whether born of truth or elaborated through years of retellings, continues to be a part of Edinburgh's haunted lore. It serves as a reminder of the eerie beauty of the Victorian Christmas—a time when people gathered around the hearth not just to warm themselves but to embrace the darkness and the stories it inspired.

CHAPTER TWENTY-THREE
THE LOST CHILDREN OF WELLESLEY

The story of "The Lost Children of Wellesley" combines elements of local folklore and the haunting atmosphere that New England towns like Wellesley are known for. The legend, set in the late 19th century, tells of two young siblings who vanished during a winter storm just before Christmas. Despite frantic searches, their bodies were not found until the spring thaw, a tragic outcome that left a deep scar on the community.

According to local lore, the children—brother and sister, ages seven and nine—were last seen playing in the snow near their family's home on the outskirts of Wellesley. It was a harsh winter, with snowstorms rolling through the area frequently, and the cold had grown bitter. On that fateful day, a sudden blizzard swept in, and the children failed to return home before dusk. As the snow thickened, their tracks vanished, making it nearly impossible for their parents and neighbors to trace them. By nightfall, word had spread throughout the town, and search parties, armed with lanterns and bundled in thick woolen coats, ventured into the dense woods surrounding Wellesley, hoping to find the children before the cold claimed them.

The search continued for days, but the combination of heavy snowfall and the unforgiving landscape proved too difficult. Some searchers reported hearing strange, faint sounds in the distance—whispers that could have been the wind or perhaps the cries of the lost children. Yet no trace of them was found. Desperate hope turned to resignation as the snow buried any chance of recovery, and the town mourned what many believed to be a senseless tragedy.

It wasn't until the following April that a hunter stumbled upon the frozen remains of the children deep within the forest, nestled in a clearing where the snow had finally begun to melt. Their bodies were discovered curled together, as if they had sought warmth in their final moments. The scene struck the townspeople with a deep sorrow, not just for the loss of young lives, but for the mystery that hung over their disappearance. How had they wandered so far from home? Why had they not called out for help that the searchers could hear?

As with many ghost stories and unexplained events, the legend of the lost children took on a life of its own. Some whispered of malevolent spirits in the woods, while others believed the children were led astray by something beyond human understanding—a figure glimpsed out of the corner of the eye, or an eerie feeling that had settled over the town that winter. Wellesley's dense forests, already filled with tales of ghosts and strange occurrences, became even more shrouded in mystery.

In the years that followed, a new legend emerged: on snowy nights in December, some townsfolk claimed they could hear the voices of children calling out in the woods. The stories varied—some said the sounds were faint and almost melodic, while others described the cries as desperate and chilling. A few individuals even reported seeing shadowy figures near the treeline, always vanishing before they could get too close.

One local woman, known for her tales of hauntings, described an encounter she had while walking home from a neighbor's holiday gathering. As she passed the edge of the forest, she heard what she thought was the wind, but as she stopped to listen, she distinguished the high-pitched sound of a child's laughter, followed by a whisper that sent a shiver through her spine. When she turned back, she saw small footprints in the freshly fallen snow that led into the woods—but no one else was there.

The story of the lost children found its way into local lore, shared by generations around fireplaces during the long New England winters. These tales gained more attention through blogs like *Ghosts in the Burbs*, which explore paranormal stories rooted in the Wellesley area. Though much of the blog's content is fictional, it captures the fascination and fear that tales like this inspire among residents and visitors alike.

Wellesley, like many towns in Massachusetts, is steeped in history and a sense of the eerie, where past and present seem to overlap. The town's landscape, with its old colonial homes and dark woods, is a natural setting for ghost stories. While no official records exist of the disappearance of children in the 19th century, the legend taps into a common thread of New England folklore: the belief that the past, especially its tragic moments, never fully fades away.

The story of the lost children is now part of Wellesley's cultural fabric, blending with other tales of hauntings and strange occurrences. It's a story that plays on the region's long history of harsh winters and isolation, when communities were small, and the wilderness was ever-present just beyond the last lamplight. While the details of the story may shift with each retelling, the essence remains the same: a reminder of how loss can echo through time, leaving traces that some claim to hear on the coldest of nights.

In the present day, those curious about Wellesley's haunted history can explore the town's darker side through tours or visit places rumored to have spiritual activity. Some believe that acknowledging these stories helps keep the past alive, while others are drawn by the thrill of possibly encountering a ghostly presence. Regardless of belief, the story of the lost children remains a powerful tale of loss, mystery, and the chilling presence of the unknown.

This legend continues to remind those in Wellesley that while time may bury the past beneath layers of snow and soil, some stories refuse to remain silent, especially when the night is dark and the wind carries the echoes of a winter long past.

CHAPTER TWENTY-FOUR
THE LEGEND OF KRAMPUS

Depiction of Krampus stealing children.

The legend of Krampus, a fearsome and devilish figure who serves as a counterpoint to the benevolent Saint Nicholas, has roots that stretch deep into ancient Alpine traditions. The name "Krampus" derives from the German word kram-

pen, meaning "claw," and he is often depicted as a
monstrous figure with horns, cloven hooves, shaggy fur, and
a grotesquely long tongue. Many folklorists trace his origins
to pre-Christian paganism in Central Europe, where he was
likely a part of rituals surrounding the winter solstice. These
early festivals were intended to chase away the lingering
spirits of winter, blending ancient beliefs in dark entities
with a desire to ensure a prosperous new season.

In these pagan rites, figures like Krampus were seen as repre-
sentations of nature's darker, wilder forces. Some traditions
suggest that Krampus is linked to Norse mythology, specifi-
cally as a descendant of Hel, the goddess of the underworld.
His presence was meant to embody the chaotic elements of
the winter season, contrasting sharply with the generosity of
figures like Saint Nicholas, who symbolized order and
charity.

As Christianity spread through Europe, the Church sought to
assimilate or suppress these ancient traditions. Rather than
being banished completely, Krampus was reinterpreted
within a Christian context. He became a companion to Saint
Nicholas, acting as a grim counterpart during the Christmas
season. Together, they would travel from house to house on
December 5th, known as Krampusnacht (Krampus Night),
before the Feast of Saint Nicholas on December 6th. While
Saint Nicholas rewarded well-behaved children with gifts,
Krampus dealt with those on the naughty list, using birch
rods or chains to threaten miscreants.

Krampus' chains, which were added in later Christian
versions of the myth, symbolize the Church's attempt to

bind and control darker pagan forces. In some interpretations, Krampus' chains and devilish appearance were meant to evoke imagery associated with the Christian Devil, further blending the fearsome pagan spirit with Christian symbolism. Over time, Krampus evolved from a purely demonic figure into a more complex character—one who, while terrifying, was part of the Christmas tradition and served to instill moral behavior among children.

Krampusnacht remains one of the most distinctive parts of this folklore. On the night of December 5th, men dressed as Krampus parade through the streets of Alpine towns, wielding chains and birch sticks. They chase both children and adults, swatting at those who come too close. The festivities are not just for children; they allow adults to take part in the chaos, with participants often fortified by local schnapps, adding a rowdy and boisterous element to the night. In some towns, the celebration is known as Krampuslauf (Krampus run), where groups of Krampuses run through the streets, creating a spectacle that is both thrilling and intimidating.

These modern celebrations maintain elements of their ancient origins, blending theatricality with the thrill of being pursued by a mythological monster. The costumes worn for Krampusnacht are typically elaborate, featuring hand-carved wooden masks, thick furs, and imposing horns. Despite efforts to ban Krampus festivities in the past—most notably in the 1920s and 1950s, when authorities in Austria tried to suppress what they saw as a corrupting influence on children—the tradition persisted and even experienced a revival in recent decades.

While Krampus may have been a relatively obscure figure in the past, especially outside Europe, he has experienced a surge in global popularity in recent years. This renewed interest began in the early 2000s, when exhibitions of *Krampuskarten*—vintage postcards depicting Krampus punishing naughty children—caught the public's eye. These cards, originally popular in Austria and Germany during the 19th century, often depicted Krampus dragging children into the underworld or beating them with birch rods. The imagery was dark and unsettling, yet the cards were part of a Christmas tradition meant to serve as a cautionary tale for children.

Krampus' modern resurgence is partly due to the rise of alternative Christmas celebrations, as people look for ways to balance the cheeriness of the season with something a little more sinister. Today, he appears in pop culture, from holiday-themed horror films to Krampus-themed parties and events across Europe and North America. Krampuslauf events, where people dress as Krampus and chase revelers through the streets, have become popular not only in traditional Alpine towns but also in cities around the world.

This transformation of Krampus from a rural Alpine tradition into a global cultural phenomenon highlights the enduring fascination with the darker side of folklore. He has become a symbol of the tension between chaos and order, punishment and reward, that is central to many Christmas traditions. Even as his image becomes more commercialized, with Krampus-themed merchandise and memorabilia, he remains a reminder of the season's roots in both light and shadow.

The role of Krampus in folklore goes beyond mere punishment. He represents a blend of ancient fears and societal norms, embodying the unpredictable nature of the winter season. While Saint Nicholas provides comfort and generosity, Krampus offers a harsher lesson—that actions have consequences. This duality has made Krampus a lasting symbol in cultures where he is celebrated, standing as a reminder that the rewards of kindness are paired with the risks of misbehavior.

Krampus' terrifying appearance, with his sharp horns and grotesque face, might serve as a physical manifestation of winter's threats, but his role is also one of maintaining balance. In many Alpine legends, Krampus is not entirely evil; he is seen as a necessary force that ensures children learn respect and obedience. His actions, although severe, aim to maintain a sense of order—mirroring the seasonal cycles where the harshness of winter eventually gives way to the warmth and light of spring.

Despite his roots in fear and punishment, the continued interest in Krampus suggests a more profound cultural resonance. As a figure who straddles the line between myth and morality, he offers an alternative perspective on the Christmas season—one that acknowledges that not every story about the holiday needs to be joyful and serene. For many, the tradition of Krampus allows a space for revelry that acknowledges the complexities of human behavior, blending fear, fun, and the thrill of the unknown.

While some criticize the commercialization of Krampus and lament the dilution of its original folklore, others see the modern celebrations as a way to keep the legend alive, evolving in response to contemporary tastes. As such, Krampus remains a dynamic figure, one who has transcended his origins to become an enduring part of holiday folklore around the world.

The legend of Krampus, with its blend of fear and festivity, stands as a testament to the rich and multifaceted nature of human storytelling. It reminds us that behind every celebration lies a history filled with shadows, waiting to emerge during the longest nights of the year.

CHAPTER TWENTY-FIVE
THE POLTERGEIST OF CWMBRAN

Nestled in the heart of South Wales, the town of Cwmbran has always been a place steeped in history and mystery. Established during the post-World War II era as a new town, Cwmbran grew rapidly, attracting families from various parts of the country. By 1992, it had developed into a bustling community, with rows of houses standing shoulder to shoulder along winding roads, cradled by the lush greenery of the surrounding valleys.

Yet, for all its modernity, Cwmbran retained an air of the ancient. Its rolling hills and nearby remnants of old Celtic settlements whispered of a time when the world was less understood—when the veil between the living and the dead seemed thinner. These stories of old spirits and mysterious happenings had long been part of the local folklore, shared over pints at the local pubs or told as cautionary tales to children who stayed out too late.

In a modest, semi-detached house on the outskirts of the town, a family of four prepared for the holiday season. The

Jenkins family—David, his wife Sarah, and their two children, Emily and Tom—were looking forward to a quiet Christmas. Their home, a quaint structure built in the 1970s, was typical of the area, with small windows that frosted over quickly in the winter and a brick chimney that curled smoke into the brisk December air.

But as the festive season approached, the Jenkins family began experiencing a series of strange events—events that would soon turn their quiet holiday into a chilling ordeal.

It began innocuously, as such things often do. In the early weeks of December, Sarah Jenkins noticed small, inexplicable occurrences. She'd find the kitchen cupboards slightly ajar when she was certain she had closed them. A glass of water, left on the dining table overnight, would be found on the counter in the morning. David shrugged these off, joking that perhaps they had a mischievous mouse with a flair for the unusual.

Yet as the days passed, the incidents became harder to dismiss. One evening, while Sarah was preparing dinner, a wooden spoon flew off the counter and clattered onto the floor. She stared at it for a moment, her heart racing, but dismissed it as her own clumsiness. But when Emily's toys began to move on their own, sliding across the living room floor without any apparent force, the family began to sense that something was amiss.

David tried to explain away the occurrences, attributing them to drafts in the house or the settling of the building's foundation. But a growing unease settled over the family, a sense that they were not alone in their home. When Tom, the youngest, claimed he heard whispers coming from the walls at night, Sarah's worry turned to dread.

As Christmas drew nearer, the disturbances intensified. Doors that had been firmly shut would swing open with a bang, as if pushed by an unseen force. The television turned on by itself in the middle of the night, blaring static that echoed through the darkened house. Shadows flickered across the walls, moving in ways that didn't match the glow from the fireplace or the glimmer of the Christmas lights.

On one particularly cold evening, David and Sarah awoke to a loud crash from the living room. Rushing downstairs, they found the Christmas tree toppled over, the ornaments shattered on the floor. Emily, clutching her blanket, swore she saw a dark figure standing beside the tree before it fell. David tried to comfort her, but the fear in his own eyes betrayed him.

Even the neighbors began to notice strange occurrences. One of them, Mrs. Llewellyn, an elderly woman who lived alone next door, mentioned hearing odd noises coming from the Jenkins' house late at night—footsteps pacing back and forth, and sometimes, a low, guttural hum that sent chills down her spine. "Sounds like something's stirring up in there," she'd say, her voice barely above a whisper.

The Jenkins family, desperate for answers, reached out to a local priest, Father Hughes. He visited the home, sprinkling holy water and reciting prayers in each room, but he, too, felt an unsettling presence lingering in the air. He advised the family to remain calm, but he could offer no clear explanation for what they were experiencing.

By the time Christmas Eve arrived, the Jenkinses were on edge, their home filled with tension instead of the usual warmth of the season. That night, they gathered in the living room, trying to distract themselves with carols and stories. The fireplace crackled, casting long shadows across the room, and for a brief moment, it felt like things might be normal again.

But as the clock struck midnight, an eerie stillness settled over the house. The air grew cold, and the fire in the hearth seemed to dim, as if a chill wind had swept through the room. Then, from above, came the sound that would haunt the family forever: the unmistakable jingle of sleigh bells, followed by the rhythmic clatter of hoofbeats on the roof.

David rushed outside, expecting to find some neighborhood prankster playing tricks, but the night was silent and still. There was no snow on the ground, no tracks in the frost, and no sign of anyone nearby. Yet the sounds continued, clear as day, reverberating through the house. Sarah clutched Emily and Tom close, her heart pounding in her chest, as the bells rang out in a discordant melody, growing louder and then fading into a whisper.

The family stayed up through the night, huddled together in the living room, waiting for the dawn. When morning finally broke, the bells and hoofbeats had stopped, leaving only a lingering sense of dread in the air.

In the days following Christmas, the paranormal activity gradually subsided. The whispers faded, the objects stayed in place, and the doors no longer slammed shut. It was as if whatever presence had been disturbing the Jenkins family had finished its work and moved on. They tried to resume their normal lives, but the fear never truly left them.

Sarah found herself glancing over her shoulder as she moved through the house, half expecting to see a shadow darting away. David spent hours inspecting the roof and attic, searching for any logical explanation for the sounds they had heard. But he found nothing—no loose shingles, no animal tracks, no signs of entry.

Emily and Tom spoke less of the strange events, though they occasionally asked their parents if they thought "the visitor" might come back next Christmas. The question sent shivers down Sarah's spine, and she always replied with a firm "no."

Word of the Jenkins' ordeal spread through Cwmbran, and soon, the family found themselves the subject of hushed conversations and speculation. Some locals believed that the haunting was a manifestation of a restless spirit, perhaps an old soul from the Celtic past seeking acknowledgment. Others suggested it was the work of a trickster entity, drawn to the heightened energy of the holiday season.

Local paranormal investigators, intrigued by the tale, visited the Jenkins' home, recording interviews and attempting to contact whatever presence had been there. But no new activity occurred, and their findings were inconclusive. Father Hughes, who had performed the initial blessing, speculated that the poltergeist might have been tied to an ancient Celtic tradition or ritual that coincided with the winter solstice and the turning of the year.

The more superstitious among the townsfolk spoke of "The Watcher of the Yule," a local legend about a spirit that traveled through the valleys during Christmastime, visiting homes that had somehow caught its attention. According to the tales, it would test the inhabitants, rewarding the virtuous with protection and bringing mischief to those it found lacking.

For the Jenkins family, these stories brought little comfort. They had lived through the fear, heard the sounds that defied explanation, and felt the chill of something otherworldly in their own home. As the years went by, they spoke less and less of that strange Christmas of 1992, but the memory lingered like a shadow, a reminder that some mysteries are better left unsolved.

The events of that Christmas Eve left the Jenkins family shaken. Sarah, usually pragmatic and level-headed, found herself questioning her own perception. She began to keep a journal of the occurrences, noting the exact times and descriptions of every odd event. The handwriting started neatly but grew more frantic as the days progressed, reflecting her rising anxiety.

David, too, found his skepticism waning. He spent hours reading about poltergeist phenomena, hoping to find some rational explanation. He even reached out to local historians, searching for any record of similar incidents in Cwmbran's past. But all he unearthed were tales of ancient spirits tied to the land, stories of spectral figures appearing in the mist-covered hills, and whispers of a "Yuletide Haunter" that visited certain homes during the darkest days of winter. The pieces did not add up, leaving David with a growing sense of dread.

Their children, Emily and Tom, were less reserved in expressing their fear. They refused to sleep in their own beds, preferring the safety of their parents' room. They spoke in hushed voices about a figure they called "the Shadow Man"—a dark silhouette they claimed to have seen flitting past their windows at night. David and Sarah tried to reassure them, but their own nerves were frayed.

Even small moments of normalcy felt like a fragile facade. The family went through the motions of Christmas—decorating the tree again, playing holiday music, and trying to fill the house with warmth. Yet every creak of the floorboards, every sudden draft, set them on edge. Sarah caught herself flinching at the sound of the wind outside, convinced that she heard faint whispers carried with it.

In their desperation, the Jenkinses agreed to a visit from a local paranormal investigation group. The team, calling themselves the Welsh Paranormal Society, arrived with an assortment of equipment—EMF detectors, infrared cameras, and audio recorders. They spent a night in the house, setting up their devices in each room, hoping to capture evidence of the disturbances.

The investigators stayed through the evening, asking the family questions about the events they'd experienced. They recorded every sound, every flicker of the lights, and even attempted to communicate with whatever presence might be lingering in the home. David and Sarah watched uneasily as the lead investigator, a middle-aged man named Rhys

Morgan, called out into the darkness, inviting any spirits to make themselves known.

For hours, nothing happened, and the team's enthusiasm began to wane. But around midnight, just as they were about to pack up, one of the motion detectors in the living room was triggered. The temperature in the room dropped suddenly, and the EMF reader spiked. The investigators recorded a faint sound—an echo of the sleigh bells and hoof-beats that had haunted the family on Christmas Eve. It was barely discernible, but it sent chills through everyone present.

When the team reviewed the footage later, they discovered something even more unsettling. In one frame of the infrared footage, a shadowy figure appeared behind the Christmas tree, barely more than a silhouette, but distinctly humanoid. The image was blurry, but the suggestion of eyes—two pinpricks of light—stared directly into the camera lens. The investigators could not provide a definitive explanation, and the Jenkinses were left with more questions than answers.

In the days following the investigators' visit, the sense of dread deepened. The activity resumed, though it never reached the intensity of Christmas Eve. Yet the knowledge that others had witnessed something abnormal in their home made it harder for the family to dismiss their experiences. The noises persisted—scratches within the walls, the occasional slamming door, and the chilling feeling of being watched.

Sarah, growing more desperate, reached out to a local historian who specialized in Welsh folklore. The historian, Mrs.

Evans, was a woman in her seventies with a passion for ancient tales. She visited the Jenkins home one cold January afternoon, carrying with her a leather-bound book filled with accounts of Welsh ghost stories and legends.

As they sat at the kitchen table, Mrs. Evans recounted tales of "The Naddredau"—spirits that roamed the valleys during the darkest nights of the year. According to legend, these spirits were drawn to homes where tension or grief lingered, feeding off the emotions of those inside. Some believed they could be warded off with offerings of bread or milk left outside the front door. Others said that they were a warning, a harbinger of change or loss.

David listened intently, clinging to the possibility that they could take some action to rid their home of the presence. But Mrs. Evans' words offered little comfort. She looked around the living room, her gaze lingering on the corners where the shadows seemed to gather. "I don't think your visitor is one of the Naddredau," she said finally, her voice low. "This feels... older, and perhaps, more personal."

As winter deepened and the days grew darker, David decided to delve deeper into the history of the house itself. He discovered that the land on which their home stood had once been part of a larger estate, dating back to the early 19th century. The estate had belonged to a local family, the Pritchards, who were known for their eccentric practices—one of which involved an old Yuletide tradition of "spirit calling." The Pritchards believed that during the winter solstice, the veil between the living and the spirit world thinned, allowing them to communicate with their ancestors.

There were no records of hauntings in the house before the Jenkins family moved in, but the idea that the land carried some spiritual residue seemed possible. David shared his findings with Sarah, and they wondered if their family had somehow become entangled in this forgotten ritual, unintentionally summoning a presence that sought to make itself known.

They considered moving, but the practicalities of work and the children's schooling made it difficult. The housing market was slow, and they feared that rumors of the haunting might deter buyers. And so, they remained, trying to adapt to a life that no longer felt like their own.

In late January, just as the cold began to ease, Sarah experienced one last, chilling encounter. She had been alone in the house, putting away the last of the Christmas decorations, when she heard a soft voice—a whisper that seemed to come from the direction of the fireplace. She froze, straining to hear the words. The voice, thin and airy, spoke in a language she did not recognize, but the tone was unmistakably mournful.

Then, just as quickly as it had begun, the voice fell silent, leaving Sarah with the lingering sense of a presence watching her. She backed away, her hands trembling, and bolted the living room door behind her. It was the last time she heard the whispers, but the memory clung to her like a shadow, a reminder that the unseen world was never far away.

As February arrived, the disturbances in the Jenkins' home finally ceased. It was as if the spirit—or whatever it had been

—had decided to leave them in peace. The air in the house felt lighter, and the shadows that had seemed so threatening began to fade with the lengthening days.

David and Sarah agreed to keep their story out of the public eye, fearing that the attention might only bring more distress. They replaced the broken ornaments and tried to rebuild a sense of normalcy, but the memory of that Christmas lingered, especially on the cold nights when the wind howled through the valley.

Emily and Tom eventually returned to their own beds, though they still preferred to leave the hallway light on. And each Christmas, Sarah continued the tradition of leaving a small plate of bread on the doorstep—an offering to whatever might be listening, just in case.

Years later, the Jenkins children grew up and moved away, but the story of the Poltergeist of Cwmbran remained a point of curiosity for those who heard it. Paranormal enthusiasts continued to speculate about the nature of the haunting, weaving theories about time slips, residual energy, or even a trickster spirit drawn by the holiday season.

The Jenkins family, however, never sought fame or validation. They kept the story among themselves, sharing it only with close friends who could be trusted to listen without judgment. For them, the poltergeist was not a source of fascination but a reminder that some things in life defy understanding.

David and Sarah would later reflect that the experience had brought their family closer together, uniting them against a shared fear. But they also carried with them the unsettling realization that in the darkest nights, even in a town as ordinary as Cwmbran, the boundaries between the known and the unknown could blur. And sometimes, just sometimes, the mysteries of the world reached out, reminding them that their cozy little home was not as isolated from the strange and the supernatural as they once believed.

————

If you enjoyed this, you may like Ethan Hayes' book:
Halloween Haunts

ABOUT THE AUTHOR

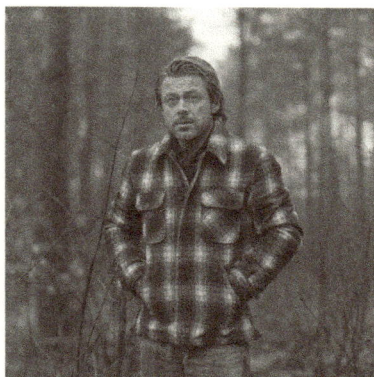

Ethan Hayes grew up in Oklahoma and moved to Texas when he attended Texas A&M. Upon graduation he was hired by Texas Parks and Wildlife and remained there until he retired twenty-two years later. He currently lives in southeast Texas with his wife and two dogs. When he's not spending time enjoying the outdoors and writing, he sips a cold beer on his front porch while listening to Bluegrass music.

Send in your encounter story: encountersbigfoot@gmail.com

ALSO BY ETHAN HAYES

www.ingramcontent.com/pod-product-compliance
Lightning Source LLC
Chambersburg PA
CBHW032111280326
41933CB00009B/794